Cause of Death: Political Correctness

*How and why political correctness
kills creativity, productivity, and children;
And what the future might be*

Yoram Solomon, PhD, MBA, LLB

Lori Vann, MA, LPC-S

© 2018

MORE FROM YORAM SOLOMON

Culture starts with YOU, not your boss!

Un-Kill Creativity

Blueprints for the Next Big Thing (2nd Ed.)

Bowling with a Crystal Ball (2nd Ed.)

From Startup to Maturity

Business Plan through Investors' Eyes

Worst Diet Ever (2nd Ed.)

MORE FROM LORI VANN

A Caregiver's Guide to Self-Injury

A Practitioner's Guide to the Treatment of Self-injury: tips, techniques, activities, and debates

The Self-injury Prevention Activity Workbook

Dedicated to the future generations.
We hope we didn't screw it up for you.

Cause of Death: Political Correctness

Table of Contents

List of Figures

Foreword by Yoram

Almost every year before Christmas, some of my Christian friends would ask me if I would be offended if they wished me "Merry Christmas" (I'm Jewish). Maybe they should wish me "Happy Hanukah," (which typically falls near the same time as Christmas) or just the generic, "Happy Holidays?" Once, speaking in front of a group of 70 high school students, I asked them to raise their hands if they had ever wished "Merry Christmas" to another person. All hands went up. Then, I asked them to keep their hands up if they ever wished that with the intent of offending the other person. All hands went down. Well, if you say something to me without the intention of offending me, the only reason I would get offended is if I chose to be offended. It would be my choice, not your fault. It's not you, it's me…

Being an elected official, the topic of political polarization bothers me a lot. On a regular basis, I experience how officials are clinging to extreme positions, just so they can emotionally appeal to their supporter base, in order to get re-elected.

My previous books and research addressed corporate culture; on many occasions, I experienced firsthand how political correctness prevented direct dialogue between employees. The "meeting *after* the meeting" and the "meeting *before* the meeting" take place, just not the meeting *during* the meeting. The inability (or unwillingness) to say what you mean for fear of consequences paralyzes Corporate America. It prevents employees from being creative. It prevents teams and companies from being innovative. And that lack of innovation causes companies to lose market share, revenue, profits, and eventually their existence.

Serving on a prominent school board, it pains me to see that our students are becoming less resilient. They are less equipped to face life than previous generations. They are being shielded from the world's realities. They need their "safe spaces," and must avoid "microaggressions."

It was those feelings that started brewing in me that caused me to start thinking about this book. And that's when I met Lori. I enjoyed spending the last several months with her refining the ideas that led to this book. Not only did Lori bring the perspective of a therapist who deals with teen self-injury and suicide every day, but the back-and-forth bouncing of ideas with her led to some of the amazing findings we made in this book.

Foreword by Lori

Some may wonder how a counselor of 20 years gets involved with a book that deals with business, politics, war, and law schools. Writing a book on political correctness was not on my radar. In fact, I was in the process of writing my fourth book on self-injury when I met Yoram. You never know how networking with people may lead to a potentially life-changing experience. In discussing my concerns about the increase in suicides and self-injury in the schools, he asked why I thought that there was a rise in the number of incidents. I had many theories based on what I have seen in my office, classes attended with peers, and research; political correctness had not been on the top of my list as one of the causes...until we started to break the issues down. I thank him for entrusting me with his idea of writing a book that fleshed out some of the concerns that we both shared.

During one of our meetings, I had told him that I often say to colleagues that many of today's problems with families, parenting, teens, and young adults can be blamed on the 1960s. Yoram dug into the events, stressors, and factors that transpired during that era that I had not thought about, but when we put everything together...it was interesting, surprising, and an a-ha moment all rolled into one as we started to connect the potential dots. It wasn't stating that the items that we discussed were absolutes or causes, but there seemed to be many correlations that emerged.

Working with Yoram has been an enjoyable and educational experience on many levels, from his insights into business, his political research, the cases that he investigated, to the many real world examples that he brought to the table. People who live and work in Ivory Towers can theorize all day as to the "what, why, how's" of this world, but it is those who have actually been in the trenches and experienced the business, educational, or counseling world first hand that would seem to have a bit more credibility when tying research together with first-hand accounts of how it played out in the "real-world." After all, are you more likely to trust the surgeon who has studied book after book on medicine, but never donned a surgeon's gown or the doctor with twenty years of experience who has performed surgeries in a variety of locations with a multitude of cases? Maybe we should develop some type of litmus test when it comes to policy development, who we vote for, or sources that we choose to listen to and follow?

This book may touch on some ideas or facts that challenge what the reader has been taught in school or in the media. Instead of shutting out these different points of view, hopefully, you can allow yourself to be challenged and to step out of your familiar world, so that you could develop a new level of understanding. Each person will have their own unique perception of things… sometimes those perceptions arouse emotions that can then contribute to some decision to act. All we ask is that you take a moment, breathe deeply a few times to make sure enough oxygen is reaching your brain, and then contemplate why do you *really* hold that opinion about a certain statement or question? From whence did your knowledge come from…family, friends, school, work, televised media, firsthand experience, hearsay, picture, video clip, bolded headline without reading the rest of the article, etc.?

May this book be a (sober) mind-opening experience that gets you a little out of your comfort zone, that challenges you at least a little, and helps you grow in a positive direction.

Introduction

We, the authors, met on August 2017 through a mutual intro-duction in the context of helping the Plano Independent School District address the ever-growing problem of teen self-injury and suicide. The conversation quickly turned into the possible sources of teens' reduced resilience that, among other issues, is a cause for those consequences. As we discussed potential causes, we realized that we both believed that Political Correctness (P.C.) played a crit-ical role in reducing that resilience. A model started emerging. By the end of that first meeting, we agreed to start working together on this book. Both of us had already published other books, but this one was going to be different from anything we previously had written.

We have different perspectives on the Political Correctness problem. Yoram is an expert on corporate innovation culture; therefore, he was mainly concerned with the impact of PC on the competitiveness of Corporate America, and America in general. Addressing the psychological facets of P.C., Lori is an expert on teen issues, self-injury, and suicide, and is mainly concerned with the impact P.C. has on those behaviors and consequences.

Throughout this book we identified several cognitive biases that humans have, such as *Confirmation Bias, Incestuous Amplification, Groupthink,* and more. Acknowledging the existence of those bias-es, we did our best to avoid them, but we are only human.

This book is non-partisan. When reading it, we hope that you would not be able to tell the party affiliation of either of us. At the same time, this book is not Politically Correct (as we defined it), nor is it apologetic about its opinions. We have absolutely no intention of offending anyone or hurting anyone's feelings. If your feelings are hurt in any way through this book, it is your choice.

The time in which we began to write this book was fraught with Political Correctness news stories. This was the time that the NFL started the kneeling protest during the singing of the National Anthem, the removing of Confederate statues all around the country, students needing "safe spaces" in colleges, and many more like events. No doubt, this book was timely.

The structure of this book

When attempting to solve a problem, you typically have to go through three steps. The first step is to determine whether it's a problem or not. The second step is to find the root cause of the problem. The third step, finally, once the answers to the first two are found, is to propose possible solutions.

This book follows the same process. The first part (2018) focuses on identifying the problem. The starting point in the first part is that Political Correctness exists, and it ties it to the devastating outcomes of loss of creativity, productivity, profitability, and life. The second part (1969) reveals the surprising causes of Political Correctness. The research for this part drew us in like no other part of that book, and it was fascinating. Finally, we took a creative approach for the third part (2034) and instead of offering prescriptive solutions, we decided to offer two alternative futures for the year 2034. Why did we choose 2034? Because it would be the 50th anniversary of *1984,* the year described in George Orwell's famous futuristic, albeit gloomy book by the same name. We both remember a time when 1984 used to be in the future…

There are two chapters in Part 3. One describes the future that could develop if we stay on the current Political Correctness trajectory (2034-A), and the other describes the future we could enjoy if we make changes (2034-B).

To set the stage, we decided to briefly quote several stories taken from recent news headlines. We did our best to cross-check those through multiple sources, and presented them in the most unbiased and objective way we could, without any commentary from us. You can skip those stories, but we encourage you to read them to see how far P.C. has reached.

Clark University

When the 2016-17 school year began at Clark University in Worcester, MA, all freshman students attended an orientation meeting. In that meeting, students were instructed to avoid subtle "micro-aggressions," and the campus vocabulary also added the terms "safe spaces" and "trigger warnings." According to the chief diversity officer at Clark University, micro-aggressions are "comments, snubs or insults that communicate derogatory or negative messages that might not be intended to cause harm but are targeted at people based on their membership in a marginalized group." Students were told never to use the phrase "you guys," as it might be interpreted as leaving out women. She also urged them never to ask an Asian student for help in math, or ask a black student if he plays basketball, as both questions make assumptions based on stereotypes and, therefore, are very offensive to women, Asians, and black students.[1]

Detroit Fire Department

Robert Pattison was a new, probationary firefighter at the Detroit Fire Department Engine 55. On September 30, 2017, Detroit Fire Commissioner Eric Jones stated that Pattison "engaged in unsatisfactory work behavior which was deemed offensive and racially insensitive to members of the Detroit Fire Department."[2] After a thorough investigation, he was terminated from the fire department. His sin? He brought a watermelon to share with his fellow firefighters. It is a tradition at Engine 55 that a new firefighter brings gifts. Those are typically doughnuts, but he could bring whatever he wanted. Pattison didn't know that bringing a watermelon would be offensive to his black colleagues. *The Atlantic* published an article explaining how watermelons became a racist trope, stating "The primary message of the watermelon stereotype was that black people were not ready for freedom."[3] Were the firefighters really offended by that watermelon? In a social media post, fellow (black) Detroit firefighter, Tadarius Spearman wrote: "Just want to let everyone know he's a real amazing dude and it was all good intentions. And our ENTIRE class [is] supporting him in this. ESPECIALLY us African-Americans and that's all that needs to be said. Stay up brother."[4] In his post, Spearman included a picture of the black fireman standing with Pattison in support. At the time of writing this book, Pattison is still fired.

Kidnapping

Dillon Reagan was working his shift at a Portland, Oregon Home Depot, when he heard a commotion outside. As he ran there, he saw a woman screaming "Somebody help me please! He's stealing my kid, he's kidnapping my child!" He called the police as the kidnapper was pulling away with the child. At the police dispatcher's request, he and a coworker followed the two until the police arrived. They gave a statement to the officers, and returned to the store, 10 minutes later. But his troubles had only begun. He was reprimanded by his supervisor for stepping away from the store for 10 minutes, saying "You did the wrong thing. You should have just gone back to work." A month after the incident, he was terminated for that decision. Once the story reached the media, and Home Depot was asked for their comments, they decided to take a second look at the decision, and reversed it, giving him back his job with back-pay.[5]

No more algebra

In a book titled *Building Support for Scholarly Practices in Mathematics Methods,*[6] an article by the University of Illinois Math education professor Rochelle Gutierrez argued that teachers should be aware of the "politics that mathematics brings" to society. A few quotes from that article, quoted by *Campus Reform:*[7]

On many levels, mathematics itself operates as Whiteness. Who gets credit for doing and developing mathematics, who is capable in mathematics, and who is seen as part of the mathematical community is generally viewed as white… curricula emphasizing terms like Pythagorean theorem and pi perpetuate a perception that mathematics was largely developed by Greeks and other Europeans.

If one is not viewed as mathematical, there will always be a sense of inferiority that can be summoned," and that minorities who "have experienced microaggressions from participating in math classrooms… [where people are] judged by whether they can reason abstractly.

Finally, Gutierrez claimed that the fact that "our economy places a premium on math skills gives math a form of "unearned privilege" for math professors, who are disproportionately white."

Indian Princess

Sachi Feris posted the following personal story in her blog, *Raising Race-Conscious Children.*[8] She told the story of how her five year-old daughter, first exposed to Disney princesses Moana and Elsa, decided to dress up as one of them for Halloween, and as the second princess the following Halloween. Feris had reservations about both costumes. She believed that Elsa (*Frozen*) defines power and privilege, carried by those who are white, with "whiteness" being the standard of beauty. Dressing up as Moana, on the other hand, she considered disrespectful when done by a white person, such as her daughter. After much arguing and protesting, her daughter finally gave in and decided to dress up as Mickey Mouse instead.

In a follow-up article[9] posted on the same blog by Lori Riddick and Feris, they offered three creeds they believed in:

1. White parents who want to dismantle White supremacy have a special burden to check their entitlement on Halloween, and make sure that their children's costume choices are not reinforcing a culture of racism.
2. Dressing up as a White person (from the dominant culture of power and privilege) is not culturally appropriate, but consider the development of children's healthy racial identities on Halloween.
3. Halloween is an opportunity to have a conversation with your child about race, power, and privilege.

****

Many fathers are familiar with the YMCA's *Indian Princesses* and *Indian Guides* programs. Those programs allow fathers to spend time and strengthen the bonds with their daughters or sons (respectively) in activities and campouts, from kindergarten age to third grade. Those activities are inspired by the Native American Indians. Some, however, failed to see that the programs respect the Native American tradition, and in turn, claimed that they are "extremely racist and offensive," and that "dads are teaching their children it's OK to patronize and (caricature) other cultures." YMCA immediately responded and removed the names and traditions of that program.[10]

And that's not all. In July 2017, a federal judge ordered the removal of trademark protection from the Washington Redskins football team, saying its name was disparaging. In addition, the California legislature voted to ban the use of the nickname by the state's high schools.

In related news, in October 2017, the Toronto School District Board decided to phase out the word "Chief" from senior staff job titles (such as *Chief Executive Officer*, *Chief Financial Officer*, etc.) "out of respect for Indigenous peoples." From now on, those titles will be replaced with terms such as "manager" and "executive officer" within the school board.[11]

Erasing history

In the three months leading to the writing of this book, the following happened:

- The Los Angeles City Council voted in August 2017 to eliminate *Columbus Day* from the city calendar, as the claim that Columbus is a symbol of genocide for Native American Indians. Don't worry, the day remains a paid holiday, but its name was changed to *Indigenous Peoples Day*. The decision passed with a 14-to-1 vote.[12]
- In September 2017, ESPN removed an announcer from the University of Virginia's first football game broadcast because of his name: Robert E. Lee.[13]
- In October 2017, the city of Austin, Texas, followed Los Angeles, and changed the name of Columbus Day to Indigenous Peoples Day in a 9-1-1 vote.[14]
- In the same month, October 2017, the *Christ Church* in Alexandria, Virginia, once attended by George Washington, who was also one of its major financiers, decided to take down the plaque honoring President Washington. "The plaques in our sanctuary make some in our presence feel unsafe or unwelcome," said leaders, referencing the fact that Washington was a slaveholder. That vote was unanimous.[15]
- Still, in October 2017, a federal appeals court ruled that a 92 years old, 40-foot cross-shaped Maryland monument honoring soldiers who died in World War I was unconstitutional because

it violates the separation between church and state as protected under the first amendment. The claim was made by the *American Humanist Association*, an organization that advocates for secularism and represented several non-Christian residents of Prince George's County. The *American Legion*, represented by the *First Liberty Institute*, a law firm that seeks to protect religious freedom plans to appeal this decision to the Supreme Court.[16]

Men's room

"Although MAN in its original sense carried the dual meaning of adult human and adult male, its meaning has come to be so closely identified with [an] adult male that the generic use of MAN and other words with masculine markers should be avoided," states a new writing guide at Purdue University. The guide further advises students to not use any words with "man" in them, such as the words mailman, man-made, congressman, or mankind. They should be replaced with words, such as "mail carrier," "machine-made," "congressional representative," or "human beings." The purpose: to write in a "non-sexist, non-biased way." The guide even adds that using those words would alienate the readers of your work, specifically women readers.[17]

In related news, Cailin Jeffers, a Northern Arizona University student, lost a point (out of 50) on an English paper she submitted because she used the sexist work "mankind." "I would be negligent, as a professor who is running a class about the human condition and the assumptions we make about being "human," if I did not also raise this issue of gendered language and ask my students to respect the need for gender-neutral language," her professor explained.[18]

We couldn't make those stories up.

Part 1: 2018
The Consequences of Political Correctness

Political Correctness Defined

We could not write a book about Political Correctness, its consequences, causes, and how to "fix" it before we clearly defined what it means.

The *Oxford Dictionary* definition of Political Correctness is:

political correctness

NOUN

> The avoidance of forms of expression or action that are perceived to exclude, marginalize, or insult groups of people who are socially disadvantaged or discriminated against.[19]

On the surface, based on this definition, there is nothing harmful in being politically correct. However, if this were the case, why did Political Correctness get such a bad reputation?

James Madison University psychology Professor Gregg Henriques wrote an essay on the issue of political correctness in *Psychology Today* magazine.[20] He defined P.C. as "the idea that many of society's ills stem from injustices based in hierarchies that were formed on the basis of sex/gender, race, and sexual orientation and that we must work to change those inequities." Again, P.C. doesn't seem negative in any way, yet. For P.C. to take place, he proposed four basic elements:

- There needs to be a recognition of hierarchy and injustice, past and present, regarding issues of gender, race, and sexual orientation;
- Those who have privilege must acknowledge that privilege and work to redress power imbalances;
- Disadvantaged individuals should point out the ways in which they were silenced, diminished, or marginalized; *and*
- Justice-loving individuals must work to undo those imbalances.

The problem is that the issues of race, gender, sexual orientation, class, and hierarchy are complex, and solving them is very complicated. P.C., however, carries the attitude of "Oppressive Righteousness," which means that "you can't share your perspective if it challenges the central tenets because you will open yourself up to charges of being an overt sexist or racist, so you end up walking on eggshells." And there lies the problem. We started confusing political correctness with respect and empathy. Those are different things. Calling out injustices and inequalities and working to close them is a good thing. But it should come out of respect and empathy for others.

Given the multiple definitions of Political Correctness, we decided to develop our own:

Political Correctness

NOUN

Relinquishing one's right and responsibility for determining appropriate and acceptable behavior and actions to people of authority.

Explanation: Instead of using our common sense to determine what's an appropriate and acceptable behavior (both our own and toward us), we use the rules we obtain from people in positions of authority (legislators, employers, schools, and media) to override our common sense.

Further explanation: We allow people in positions of authority to tell us what is considered acceptable and appropriate behavior. Not only how we should avoid offending others, but also when we should be offended by others. As a result, we stop using our common sense to make those determinations, and like any other skill, when we don't use it—we lose it.

As we tried to define P.C. for the purpose of the book, we considered several additional definitions, focused on how P.C. is being practiced:

- The focus on *saying* the right thing over *doing* the right thing;
- The focus on not offending others, rather than not allowing yourself to be offended;
- Lowering the bar for winning, rather than encouraging competition and excellence;
- The focus on creating rules rather than promoting common sense; *and*
- The distance between what you mean and what you say.

We have to clarify a point here. This definition is *our* definition of Political Correctness. Others may not agree with it. We found ourselves getting into disagreements over whether Political Correctness is a good or a bad thing. We refer to what some people call Political Correctness as respect, consideration, and empathy. We support those values wholeheartedly. Whether we should call our definition any other name, so as to not confuse current uses of the term, is a different question. We chose to refer to Political Correctness per our definition above.

History of Political Correctness

The first documented use of the phrase "Politically Correct" appeared in the Supreme Court Chief Justice John Marshall's decision in the *Chisholm v. Georgia* case in 1793 (no, that's not a typo).[21] He said:

> Sentiments and expressions of this inaccurate kind prevail in our common, even in our convivial, language. Is a toast asked? 'The United States,' instead of the 'People of the United States,' is the toast given. This is not politically correct.

The meaning was completely different than it is today. Being Politically Correct meant that it was the way politicians, the elite (the term is not used in a negative way), were to behave and speak.

In the 1960s, during the civil rights and feminist revolutions, the term was used by both political parties but, again, as a positive term. Republicans believed that the anti-war protests were Politically Incorrect, while Democrats believed that supporting the civil-rights legislation was politically correct. Both sides strived to be Politically Correct because it was considered a good thing.

Only in the late 1990s, did the definition of Political Correctness take a negative turn. It became used ironically, satirically, and sarcastically. At the same time, it became "owned" by the left, but despised by the right.

Another source for the history of the term can be found in an essay published by *Accuracy in Academia* ("a non-profit research group based in Washington, D.C. that wants schools to return to their traditional mission-the quest for truth"—taken from their website).[22] AIA believes that Political Correctness emerged from Marxism and was translated from an economic term into a cultural term, and rather than originating in the 1960s, it actually dates back to World War I. It further claims that both Marxism and Political Correctness are totalitarian ideologies, and that Political Correctness is practiced on college campuses,

> … where the student or faculty member who dares to cross any of the lines set up by the gender feminist or the homosexual-rights activists, or the local black or Hispanic group, or any of the other sainted "victims" groups that P.C. revolves around, quickly find themselves in judicial trouble. Within the small legal system of the college, they face formal charges – some star-chamber proceeding – and punishment.

One more source of historical background of Political Correctness comes from the *Claremont Institute*, an organization that "seek[s] to reinvigorate the public mind by returning to the first principles of distinctively American conservatism."[23] It claims that the origins of P.C. came from communists in the 1930s "as a semi-humorous reminder that the Party's interest is to be treated as a reality that ranks above reality itself." Things were either correct or politically correct, and the latter was more important than the former. According to that essay, P.C. was based on the concept of "cultural hegemony" that was coined by Antonio Gramsci (1891-1937), a theoretician who envisioned how totalitarianism would eliminate any possibility of cultural resistance to progressivism.

When presenting a position, it is important to show both sides of it, and while two of the sources cited here appear to be rooted in Conservative viewpoints, there is one that offers a Liberal viewpoint. Anna Szilagyi offered a linguistic explanation of the term Political Correctness in her November 2016 blog post *"Political Correctness Wanted Dead or Alive—A Rhetorical Witch-Hunt in the US, Russia, and Europe."*[24] She defined Political Correctness as "a neutral, descriptive reference to the principle of avoiding utterances and actions that can marginalize or offend certain groups of people." She also explained that due to the normative nature of the word "correctness," the use of it radiates authority and can evoke the feeling of being talked down to. She furthermore claimed that Political Correctness is used as an extravagance, as elitism, as an obsession, as intimidation, as censorship, and as deception.

One of the most powerful conclusions of her article is that "those who would like to stick with the ideals of political correctness, should consider giving a new name to their cause. Political correctness might not be what they mean anymore."

What Do YOU Think?

As the meaning of the term Political Correctness changed over the years, so have people's attitudes toward it. In this chapter we provided the results and conclusions of several polls conducted on the topic in recent years.

Between June 7 and July 5, 2016, *PEW Research* surveyed 4,602 American adults at random.[25] The main question asked was (with the results in brackets):

> Which comes closer to your own views – even if neither is exactly right?
>
> ☐ People need to be more careful about the language they use to avoid offending people with different backgrounds [39%]
> ☐ Too many people are easily offended these days over the language that others use [59%]

Only 2% did not respond. The results show a clear preference towards the second option—believing that people are offended too easily. We will revisit this study later, as there are interesting political, racial, and gender differences in how respondents answered this question.

✳✳✳

From September 24 to 26, 2017, *FOX News* conducted a telephone poll of 1,017 registered voters.[26] The poll covered many different topics, from President Trump's job performance approval to the economy, immigration, Russia, Obamacare, and more. For this chapter, we will provide the results of several questions from that poll.

- ☐ *Question 45:* 66% responded that Political Correctness has gone too far, while 23% said it didn't;
- ☐ *Question 46:* 83% believed that people behave worse in public today than 10 years ago. Only 9% believed that people behave better;
- ☐ *Question 47:* 78% believed that people are *less* courteous in the U.S. today than 10 years ago. 10% believed people are more courteous; *and*
- ☐ *Question 48:* 81% believed that the bonds that hold our nation together are weakening, while only 12% believed they are strengthening.

Finally, a *Rasmussen Reports'* August 2017 national telephone survey of 1,000 American adults showed the following results:[27]

- ☐ 85% of American adults think that giving people the right to free speech is more important than making sure no one is offended by what others say, while only 8% think it's more important to make sure no one gets offended;
- ☐ 73% agree with Voltaire's 18th century statement: "I disapprove of what you say but will defend to the death your right to say it," while only 10% disagreed with that statement; *and*
- ☐ The agreement on those attitudes was consistent across the major parties and races.

Oddly enough, those two attitudes stand in contrast with one another. On one hand, we prefer that people avoid offending each other. We prohibit the use of certain words, expressions, or actions. However, at the same time, we insist on our constitutional right to express them. Why?

Left Brain, Right Brain

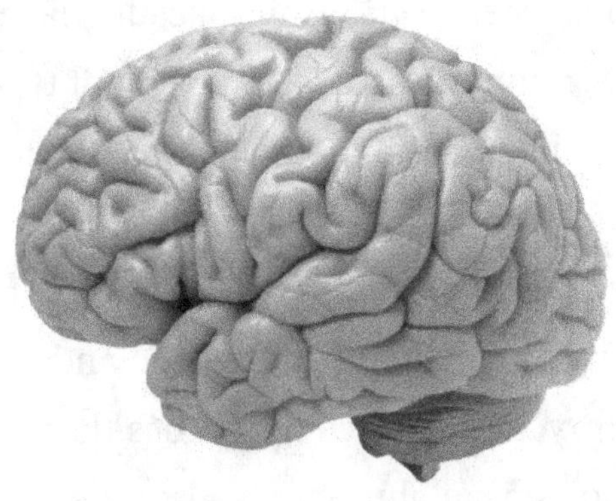

Figure 1: The human brain

Magnetic resonance imaging (MRI) of 1,000 people revealed that the human brain doesn't actually favor one side over the other. The networks on one side aren't generally stronger than the networks on the other side. Whether you're performing a logical or creative function, you're receiving input from both sides of your brain.[28]

"[T]he ability to understand what we read or what someone is saying to us requires both hemispheres, working together and separately."[29]

It is only for simplicity's sake that we are asking that you view the brain as two distinct sections instead of a brain that uses both hemispheres to make logical or emotional decisions. It is not trying to imply or state as fact that one side of the brain is the "logical" side and the other the "emotional side."

We are complicated creatures that are influenced by genetics, family interactions, peer relationships, academia, occupational history, exposure to traumatic events, media of all types, the substances that we ingest, our nutrition, our physical environment, culture, race, religion, and so many more variables. Each time we experience or learn something new, it may leave an impression on us, literally and figuratively. It is now understood and widely accepted in the medical and psychological communities that a traumatic event, such as physical or sexual abuse, may alter the sizes of the Hippocampus and Amygdala, which are located in the part of the brain that is at the back of the head. However, non-physically threatening events can also leave a lasting impression on humans, and that may lead to anything from bias to complete avoidance, or even a hatred toward anything or anyone that reminds the emotionally wounded party of the event.

You may ask, "How does this apply to political correctness?" That would be a fair question. How does neurology and psychology connect into something that we associate with angry news commentators, political motives, helping the "little guy," national court cases, sensationalized headlines, and/or rioting? This is where viewing the brain, or even the whole person, as having two sections or sides, may be helpful. Here are a few examples of how we can sometimes feel "unbalanced," and some possible implications of that feeling.

Sometimes we choose to use our "emotional" side, even though we have a "gut feeling" that we should not be engaging in that activity, such that we may regret the action we take. We can let the "heat of the moment" take over the more logical, analytical, and judicious side. Have you ever made a decision based upon how someone would feel instead of what you believed was the better course of action? Sometimes you do that to avoid conflict or "spare someone's feelings," but to the detriment of your own. In that moment, your brain is trying to decide which is the greater benefit—be correct and have someone upset with you, or worry more about feelings and risk future problems? This is the internal debate between your two sides—logical versus emotional, and it is one that takes place on a daily basis and may be completely unaware to us, i.e. unconscious. Maybe interjecting an example from the past may help better explain the concept.

Do you remember the cartoons from the 1950s and 1960s that depicted the struggle between good versus evil, where a character had a devil on one of his shoulders and an angel on the other? Each one was actively vying for his side to be the one chosen by the tormented individual. The devil was making his side seem appealing while the angel tried to remind the character of what was the correct, responsible thing to do. Sometimes the devilish side would win; when consequences arose and things became uncomfortable for the character, he looked for a way to avoid the discomfort. Often times, the character would imply or utter the phrase, "the devil made me do it," as if that would abdicate him of the consequences of his decisions.

Too often in the counseling office, therapists hear patients trying to find some "devil" to blame their actions upon instead of taking ownership of their decisions. Unfortunately, society has provided numerous examples of high-profile people, celebrities and politicians alike, who are quick to point the finger at everyone else as the reason why they decided to say or do something, instead of taking full ownership of their words and actions. In some instances, it is only after much pressure or more evidence comes out, that the person takes responsibility, but at that point, you would have to question the sincerity of the admittance. You have to wonder what impact this type of role modeling has on our society.

So when people try to abdicate their responsibility for their actions by blaming it on someone or something else, is it a sign of emotional immaturity or a lack of cognitive development? Does this tendency relate in any way to political correctness? The answer is both "yes" and "no."

Many decisions in life require a balanced thought process, one that takes into account all of the healthy, safe, and positive things that can come from making a rational decision, while acknowledging that the "devilish" side may look more enticing and even, initially, the easier path to take. It is often our emotions that will keep us in the immediate present, while often ignoring the potential future consequences, whether intentionally (burying our head in the sand) or unintentionally (emotional blinders placed over our eyes).

There are times when even if there is some type of acknowledgment of the long-term consequences by a party or a group that the temptations of the short-sighted, "in the moment," "easier path," "what's in it for me" mindset manifest themselves. As with most things, there are exceptions, such as decisions made out of truly selfless reasons where the person makes a sacrifice in order to help another person or cause; this could be seen as an emotionally based decision. Not all emotionally based decisions are short-sighted, unhealthy, or bad; some make people heroes, such as the case of teachers who shield students from gunfire with their own bodies, or soldiers who voluntarily enlist and serve in active combat.

One of the founding fathers of psychology, Sigmund Freud, theorized that we have three parts of the psyche involved in decision making—the *Id*, the *Ego*, and *Superego*. When people choose an immediate reward that only pleases themselves, it's said that they let their Id make the self-gratifying decision. The key here is the intent; the Id's intent is only about the pleasure of the person and does not consider another's needs. Let's think of a baby who wants to be fed immediately, regardless of the environment or timing. We would say that their Id was in charge. Some adults that have been encountered in the counseling world that have narcissistic, anti-social, or borderline tendencies could be said to have their Id as their decision maker. When political correctness creates negative results, could it be that man took an initially good intent idea and changed it into a self-gratifying cause (financial gain, power, prestige) that only benefits a few while harming the majority?

The Ego is the middle state that seeks balance between the "free for all, what's in it for me" mindset of the Id, and the highly moral Superego that may only see things in black and white, with no gray areas, or only as a "right or wrong" issue with no exceptions to the rules. In counseling, patients are often encouraged to avoid the extremes in decision making; rarely does going to extremes pan out for the patient or those around them. Extremism can give us tunnel vision or even observation bias. Instead, patients are encouraged to find some form of "happiness in the middle," since rarely are there situations that are 100% one way with no exceptions. This is where you need a logical and an emotional side, thus the Ego. Those who haven't developed these three levels, Id, Ego, and Superego, may be considered emotionally stunted.

In counseling sessions, patients are often encouraged to remember the phrase, "short-term benefits, long-term consequences." It is encouraging them to not make impulsive or emotionally based decisions that may lead to anticipated and unanticipated problems in the near or distant future. Often times, when someone is in an emotional state, it can be difficult for them to make a clear, objective, rational decision. They wish to ease the emotional discomfort as quickly and expeditiously as possible; thus, a quick, not well-thought out decision may ensue. The same effect may occur in politics when there is pressure placed on Congress to act upon a piece of legislation in a rushed manner without conducting full due-diligence. The quote, "we have to pass it to know what's in it" comes to mind.

What may seem convenient and maybe a "just this time" exception or an "it is no big deal" mindset may create the precedent for significant change that alters a society. Is it possible that some of the issues that we consider to fall under the "P.C." category started with this type of mindset? The decision may have been made out of "good intentions," but without thinking through all of the possible implications, the "good intention" may result in an unforeseen negative outcome. One might even think of the old proverb, "The road to hell is paved with good intentions."

No Punching Below the Belt

To explain how Political Correctness affects your behavior, we chose to use the boxing analogy. One of the rules in boxing is—no punching below the belt.

How does that apply?

The belt is analogous to our sensitivity threshold. We can handle anything you throw our way as long as it is *above* the belt. But we really get hurt if you punch us *below* the belt.

Our communication and discourse are made of three elements: the words that we use, our tone of voice, and our body language.[30] Each one of those has elements that are "above the belt" and elements that are "below the belt."

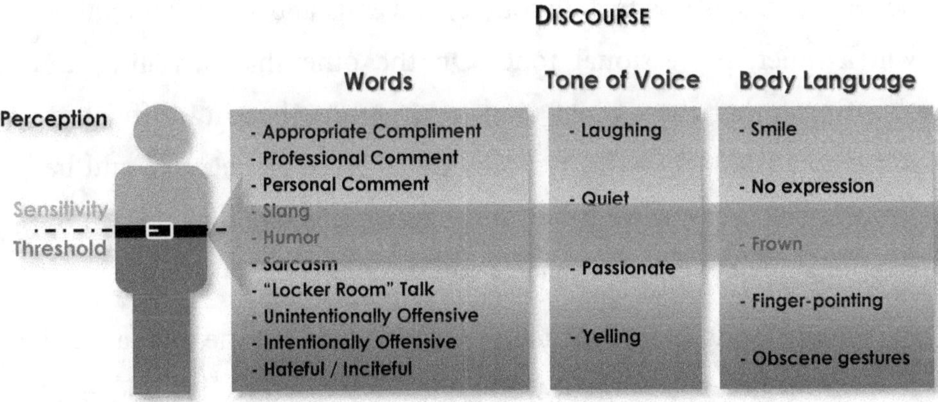

Figure 2: Discourse, sensitivity level, and the belt

Take words, for example. A professional comment made from one person to another would typically be considered above the belt. An appropriate compliment would be further above the belt (keep in mind, though, that in this age of Political Correctness, a compliment might be interpreted as an unwelcome sexual advance, so beware…). On the other hand, hateful and inciteful words are definitely below the belt. Words said with an intention to offend the listener are below the belt, too.

But there are words that are much closer to the belt. Personal comments, slang, and humor could still be considered above the belt, but in some cases, they might be perceived as offensive. Sarcasm can be great among friends who trust each other, but might be perceived negatively by others who are not as close to you.

You must feel very comfortable with someone, probably of the same sex as you, to be using "locker-room" talk. And best if you are not recorded…

The same applies to the tone of voice. Laughter would typically be considered as positive discourse, and thus above the belt, and so will a quiet, professional tone. On the other hand, yelling and shouting (other than when used to overcome hearing difficulties, noise, or distance) would typically be received as negative and below the belt. Passionate tone? Well, again, this one depends on the relationship between the speaker and listener.

Finally, body language can be on both sides of the belt, as well. A smile, or no expression, would typically be perceived as above the belt, and thus not offend anyone. Finger pointing, being "in your face," and making obscene gestures would definitely be below the belt.

***

For this part, we assume that both sides of an interaction are "normal" and have their "belts" (or sensitivity threshold) right where they should be—at the waistline.

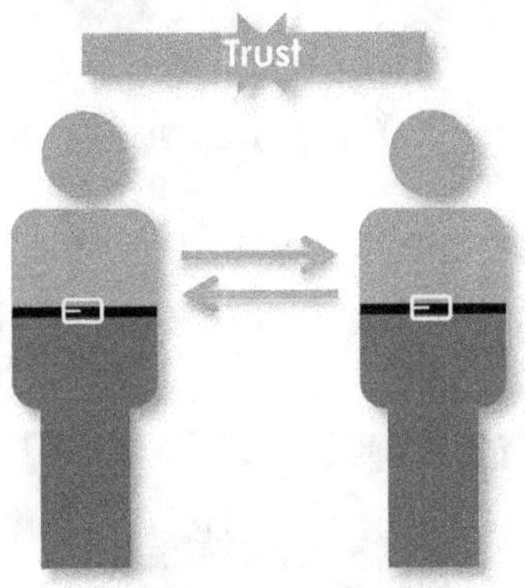

Figure 3: Rational, constructive interaction

When the two speak above the belt, they listen to each other, they think before they speak, they use the rational side of their brain, and they conduct a rational, constructive interaction.

Positive interactions bring people together. The more positive, intense, and frequent those interactions are, the faster trust will build between the two sides. When trust builds, the "belt" goes lower, and they can accept as normal interactions that would have typically be considered offensive. Sarcasm would be one example.

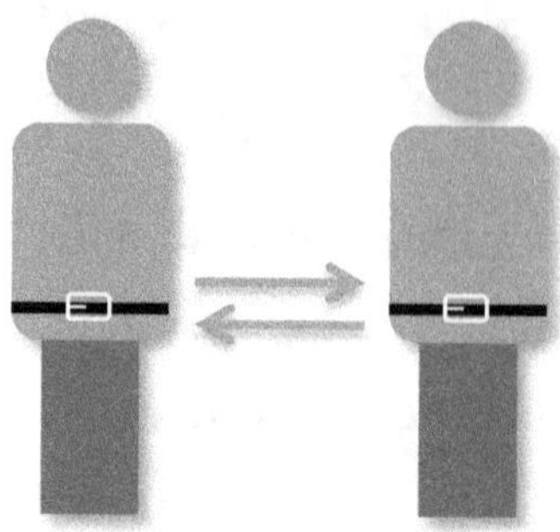

Figure 4: Trust-full interactions

On the other hand, when we start punching below the belt, it hurts. And when it hurts us, we punch back… below the belt.

Figure 5: Emotional, irrational interaction

The principle of reciprocity forces us to do so. In fact, we expect more from others than we do from ourselves, for the most part. Think about this: you are driving, and you see the car in front of you not keeping in its lane. You know what's happening. You pass them, and sure enough—the driver is texting. What do you feel? This driver has not only put himself in danger, but also you! Not to mention the annoyance of driving slower than the speed limit and delaying you. Such lack of respect, right?

Well, do you ever text and drive? Don't answer that—it's not legal in quite a few states. But, do you? Why do you expect others to respect you more than you respect them?

Don't worry—you are not alone.

Arizona State University psychology professor Robert Cialdini showed many examples of responding positively to positive gestures towards you. However, the same is true for negative gestures. Barbara Frederickson's Broaden and Build Theory of Positive Emotions[31] states that we respond three times stronger to negative emotions than to positive ones.

The interaction below the belt doesn't hit our brain at the rational side. It hits the emotional, irrational side. We don't listen anymore. We entrench ourselves in our inflexible positions. We are affected more by *confirmation bias* and *incestuous amplification* (both will be explained later). When that happens, things escalate quickly. Trust gives way to adversity and polarization.

***

This would be a good time to suggest another possibility—that the person who punched below the belt did so *unintentionally*.

Figure 6: Unintentionally offensive interaction

How can one punch the other below the belt unintentionally? When you don't know someone, you tend to make assumptions. You may make a joke that would be funny to 99% of the population, but just not to the person you are speaking with. There is almost nothing you can't joke about, but some people might be more sensitive to certain issues. Different people also come from different cultures. Certain hand gestures might be completely harmless and playful in one culture, but try to make those same gestures to a person from another culture, and you would offend them. Either way, the less you know someone, the more likely you are to unintentionally offend them.

The outcome, as unintentional as it might be, is negative. The other side punches back, below the waistline. You might be surprised at this reaction, but nevertheless, you will respond as you would to a punch below your own belt. You would punch back.

Finally, some people are simply not sensitive enough to know what's appropriate and what's not. For example, someone who is diagnosed on the Autism spectrum would simply not pick up on cues that indicate the other person's sensitivity to certain words, tone, or gestures.

When sharing the ideas for this book with others, one of the most consistent pieces of feedback we received was from people who associated being politically correct with being respectful. We go back to our definition of Political Correctness. Being less politically correct doesn't mean you should be disrespectful or ignorant. You still have the responsibility to be respectful, to get to know the people you are interacting with, to learn their "hot buttons" and avoid pressing them.

In comes Political Correctness. Perhaps the best way to describe its effect is through a cartoon about, you guessed it, boxing.

Figure 7: No punching below the belt

Since no punching below the belt is allowed, one of the boxers pulls his pants over his head, making his entire body "below the belt."

And that is exactly what Political Correctness does. The following diagram illustrates that effect. In the middle is the "normal" person, with "normal" sensitivity threshold, wearing his belt where he should—at his waistline. Political correctness causes people to raise their belt, almost to the point of pulling their pants over their heads. The higher the belt is, the more interactions become "below the belt" punches. And remember, what is it that we do when we are punched below the belt? We punch back!

Figure 8: Political correctness and the sensitivity threshold

Political Correctness doesn't tell you to raise your own belt; instead, it tells you that you should assume that the other person has his belt higher, and thus, you should avoid punching them even higher than their waistline.

However, a side effect of being more sensitive to others is becoming more sensitive yourself. If you can't say something to the other person then, by God, he can't say that to you! Not only that we become more sensitive not to offend others, but we become more easily offended ourselves!

The same interaction that is above the belt for "normal" people is now below the belt. A compliment is interpreted as a sexual advance. A simple act of bringing a watermelon to work becomes a racially motivated and highly offensive act, which would cause termination of employment. Makes sense, doesn't it? In essence, P.C. takes away us giving people the benefit of the doubt.

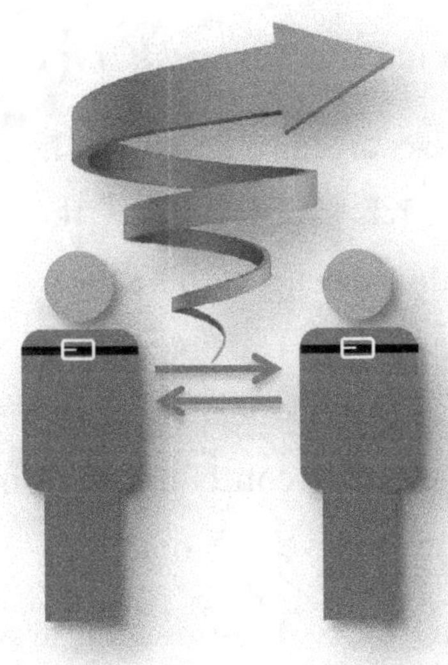

Figure 9: P.C. Effect on an, otherwise, rational interaction

As the above diagram shows, what should have been rational and positive is now considered negative, emotional, and personal. What should have promoted trust, now promotes adversity and polarization.

And what happens if the conversation actually takes place at the small area that is left above the belt?

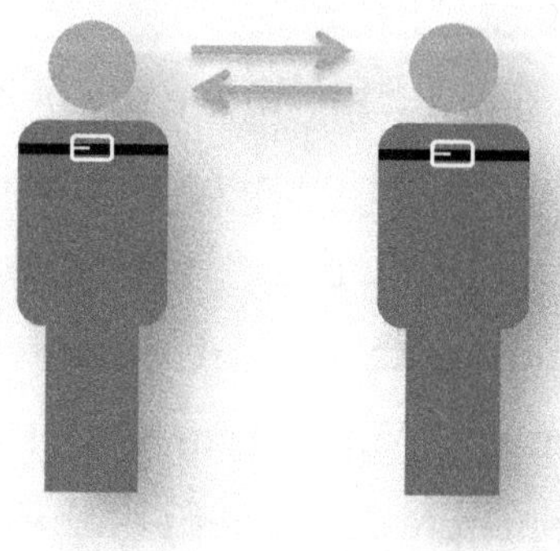

Figure 10: The only rational politically correct interaction

In this case, more is unsaid than said. The conversation is highly Politically Correct. Each side feels that the other is not genuine. Trust erodes. You don't believe the other person. You hold "the meeting before the meeting" to coordinate positions, and then you hold "the meeting after the meeting," where decisions are really made. The meeting itself is content-free. It is very civil, peaceful, but is it productive or creative? It's not!

We will cover one more one-on-one interaction here. The one that takes place when one person is "normal" (wearing his belt at the waistline) while the other is significantly Politically Correct (wearing his belt very high).

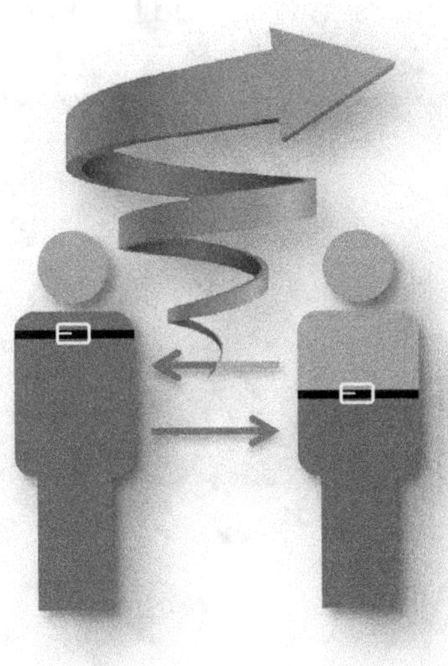

Figure 11: P.C. mismatch interaction

In this scenario, the "normal" person says something to the other that should be acceptable to him, not realizing that the other person, forced by Political Correctness, has his belt (or sensitivity threshold) higher than normal, and would interpret your benign words, tone, or gestures as offensive. As a result, he would punch back. Below *your* belt. And what would you do? You guessed it—you would punch back!

***

Janus

And just when you thought that we have you all figured out, there is another dimension to your personality. Janus is the Roman god of beginning, gates, transitions, time, *duality*, doorways, passages, and endings.[32]

He has a unique characteristic: he has two faces. So do we. So do you.

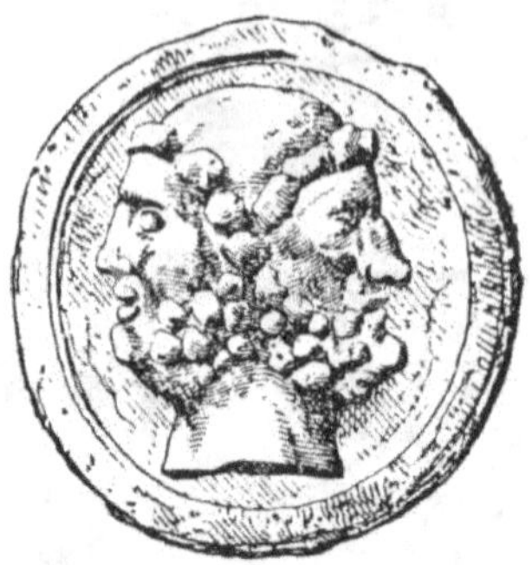

Figure 12: Janus coin

To this point, our description of interactions assumed that people have only one type of behavior, depending on their level of Political Correctness (where their belt is). However, that is not the case. In reality, we treat different people differently. In his book, *The Brain*, author David Eagleman described an experiment designed to answer the question of whether the basic sense of empathy will change with the identity of the person you interact with. Specifically, if that person is a member of your "in-group" (the group of "your" people, or "people like you") or "out-group" (people who are not "your" people, or "people not like you").

For that experiment, they showed two images to participants. The images were of a hand. In one image, the hand was stabbed with a syringe needle, and in the other, the hand was touched with a cotton swab. As the participants watched those images, their brains were scanned by an MRI machine. The scan showed that when they saw the image of the hand being stabbed, the pain matrix in their brain was activated, as if they were being stabbed themselves. This is what we call *empathy.*

This first step of the experiment has established the baseline of how the participants responded differently to images of pain versus images of no pain.

In the second step, there were 6 images of hands, but this time with a one-word label next to each one: Christian, Jewish, Atheist, Muslim, Hindu, or Scientologist. Those selections assured that each participant would consider one (or more) to be in their in-group, while one (or more) would be in their out-group.

A hand was randomly selected and brought to the center of the screen (with its label). Then the hand was shown to be touched with the cotton swab, followed by being stabbed with the needle. The results showed dramatic differences. If the hand belonged to a person in the participant's in-group (based on the label next to it), the empathic response was significantly higher than if the hand appeared to belong to someone in the participant's out-group. For the latter, the empathic response was significantly lower.

The same applies to Political Correctness. We will wear the belt at different heights depending on the person we are interacting with, and whether they are part of our in-group or part of our out-group.

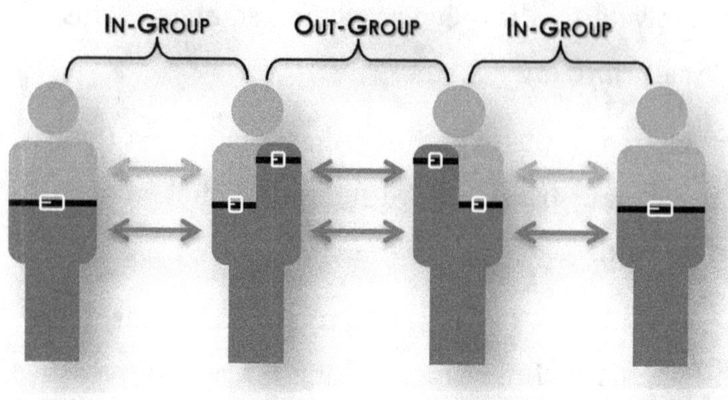

Figure 13: In-Group and Out-Group interactions

From someone in our in-group, we are willing to accept ideas or behaviors that we would absolutely not be willing to accept from someone in our out-group. At the same time, we feel more comfortable saying (or doing) certain things to people in our in-group that we would not imagine doing to someone in our out-group.

In one of our interviews with a teacher, he told us that he and his students were forbidden from calling an African-American student a Negro. This word was deemed racially inappropriate and highly offensive to black people. However, he complained, the black students in his classroom called each other a Negro. They felt more comfortable calling each other that, feeling part of each other's in-group, but would not tolerate hearing it from someone in their out-group.

***

When Political Correctness forces us to be more sensitive to others so that we would avoid offending them, it also forces us to perceive more things as offensive to us. It becomes simply too hard to interact with others, so we begin to keep our distance from them. Several psychological effects take place. Generally, you can refer to them as "don't bother me with the facts—I've already made up my mind…" In professional terms, they are called *Confirmation Bias* and *Incestuous Amplification.*

Don't bother me with the facts

On August 6, 2007, in a blog post[33] he has not kept publicly accessible in his archives, R. Scott Clark wrote the following concerning the Federal Vision (FV) controversy:

> Remember, since the 16th century, revisionists and errorists have always said, 'We're just following the Bible.' That was the loudest refrain of the Socinians, who ended up denying the Trinity. They denied the deity of Jesus, the substitutionary atonement and justification by works all on the ground that, they were just following the Bible. All heretics quote Scripture. The question in this controversy is not the normativity of the Bible but who gets to interpret it.
>
> Thus in some circles there is the desire to require officers (sometimes even members) to subscribe to every proposition in the church's confession. And if the ground of their authority is your agreement with their interpretation of Scripture, that is the equivalent of painting the magisterial target around your interpretive arrow. Then phrases like 'the Westminster Standards set the boundaries for us' and 'confessionally bound' [to the WCF] are misleading, because then ultimately it is your own interpretation that is setting the boundaries, and you are picking the confession that matches your own interpretation.

Imagine two people going to the same movie, both are paying attention and not on their phones or asleep. At the end of the movie, both share their perceptions of the film, such as the theme, the message, was the actor the best fit for that role, etc. Each person has a different answer to the questions. Does this mean that one person is right and the other is wrong? Maybe on some questions there might be a clearer right/wrong response, but what about those that are more interpretive or subjective? We often fall into the trap of believing somehow our perception or interpretation is the only correct one. While "majority rule" is sometimes correct (how else would we develop diagnoses if not for looking at what is "normal" the greatest percentage of the time), it is not an absolute. When the minority or dissenting opinion is not taken into account, we miss the value in better understanding another person on a deeper level, how not all policies can be a "one size fits all," or that there are often "exceptions to every rule."

Figure 14: Don't bother me with the facts

We do not live on a planet where everyone was raised the same way with the same education system, religious upbringing, parenting styles, economic status, role models, or exposure to trauma. All of these, and many more factors, influence how we see the world, the rules for our lives, and how we will deal with them. Given those factors, some individuals may not be consciously aware of a bias that interferes with their ability to recognize some "rules" as facts, as based upon the numerous criteria that comprise calling something a fact.

While it may be the punch line to a situation, unfortunately, some people may live in a world where they "do not want to be bothered by the facts" of that situation. On the surface, this seems highly illogical, but let's hypothesize how some people get to this level. Could it be that doing the research is too tedious? Perhaps they do not understand the research or the concepts being addressed? Maybe they are poor historians and do not remember past experiences. Maybe it is a time issue where they do not have the time to look up the information? Could they be impressionable and follow other people's opinions instead of developing their own through critical thinking? While it may be far more convenient to "ignore the facts" and create our own reality to justify our actions, it is not the reality that the rest of the world deals with on a daily basis. To go back to Scott Clark's quote, "ultimately it is your own interpretation that is setting the boundaries, and you are picking the confession that matches your own interpretation."

We tend to think that our interpretation is the only correct one, which forces us to only seek out opinions or "evidence" that corresponds with our opinion. These are clear biases. While on the surface this may seem benign, when extended out, it may lead to a concept called *incestuous amplification.*

Paul Krugman is a distinguished professor of economics at the Graduate Center of the City University of New York, a Nobel Prize laureate in economics, and a columnist for the New York Times. Here he explains the potential dangers of this bias:

> I learned that the military has a term for how highly dubious ideas become not just accepted, but viewed as certainties. "Incestuous amplification" happen[s] when a closed group of people repeat the same things to each other – and when accepting the group's preconceptions itself becomes a necessary ticket to being in the in-group. A fundamentally flawed notion – say, that the Germans can't possibly attack [through] the Ardennes – becomes part of what everyone knows, where "everyone" means by definition only people who accept the flawed notion.
>
> And at this point, of course, all the Very Serious People have committed their reputations so thoroughly to the official doctrine that they almost literally can't hear any contrary evidence.[34]

This type of situation can occur in academic, media, religious, and political circles. Per the previous article discussing two groups of the same denomination with different perspectives, "*All heretics quote Scripture. The question in this controversy is not the normativity of the Bible but who gets to interpret it.*" The scarier proposition is that those who think that they alone get to choose, or dictate, the interpretation of some issue or policy may fall to the human nature struggle with becoming power hungry.

Humans, whether we like it or not, have a long history of falling prey to the temptations of being powerful and elite. It strokes our egos because we like to feel "special;" after all, haven't advertising companies done much work on developing programs for their clients to help with customer retention based upon making the customer feel "special," "unique," valued" with access to "membership only" deals? And what is one of the most elite circles to run in? Government. They influence and set the rules for an entire country. Some politicians appear to be more concerned with keeping their seat of power and influence, and the lobbyists play into that greed. When lobbyists are influencing politicians with the agenda that they want to have passed through, then sometimes the "don't bother me with the facts" situation arises. At another level, any politician on the fence about something may be swayed with the "incestuous amplification" by hearing their colleagues or President state the same information over and over and over again until it "sounds good" or "seems to make sense" without actually looking at the facts.

In his explanation of how highly intelligent men approved the stupid plan that created the Watergate debacle, Arizona State University Professor Emeritus of Psychology and Marketing Robert Cialdini claims that John Mitchell, Jeb Magruder, and John Dean approved G. Gordon Liddy's foolish plan (in their own words in a later testimony) because he made two concessions before he made the final proposal, while Frederick LaRue was not privy to those concessions.[35] However, could it be that Mitchell, Magruder, and Deal approved the plan simply because they already head it for the third time, and at that point it started to make sense to them, while

LaRue was only hearing it for the first time, thus not yet suffering from incestuous amplification?

***

Have you ever thought about how you use the words *Conservative*, *Liberal*, *Progressive*, and the like? Those three words are defined by the Oxford dictionary, Merriam-Webster dictionary, and dictionary.com as *adjectives*.[36] But do we use them as such? Do we say that someone is conservative, or do we say that she is *A* Conservative (a noun)? Do we say that someone is liberal, or that he is *A* Liberal? Think about the difference. When you use any of those words as they were intended to be used, as adjectives, you are referring to one of *many* characteristics of that person. However, when you use them as nouns, you essentially define that person as that word. That person stops becoming a person and instead becomes a conservative. A *thing.* And when we refer to people as things, we further the dehumanization of them.

Of course, we also label ourselves with those words when used as nouns. At election time, look at campaign signs. How many candidates identify themselves as *a* Conservative or as *a* Liberal? And if we belong to one box, while others belong to the other box, we further the separation between the in-group and out-group that we mentioned before, and will be mentioned again in this book.

***

Several factors come into play here that force us to see the world in black-and-white. It is so much easier to categorize or label people into one of two boxes. It's a shortcut that our brain makes. You are either in one box, or the other, and I know everything there is to know about you, simply by knowing which box you "belong" to. If you are Republican (*A* Republican), then you are socially conservative, fiscally conservative, pro-life, anti-gay, pro-second amendment right to bear arms, etc. If you are *A* Democrat, you are progressive, socially liberal, pro-gay rights, pro-choice, pro-strict gun control, etc. And that's that. We don't need to think any further. All I have to know is one single fact about you that will help me know exactly which box (out of two) you belong to, and then I know everything about you. Or, do I?

Drew Smith, who holds a PhD in Molecular, Cellular and Development Biology, described in a response to a question,[37] that each human being carries some 13,500 variants of DNA exomes, 300 of which affect gene functions. As a result, he believes that the number of possible DNA combinations would be 1 x 2 x 3 ... x 300, which equals to 3×10^{614}. It's a very large number. But it tells you something very important—we are all different. We cannot simply label people in only one of two labels. We do it because it's convenient. Not for any other reason. But you do it anyway. As a result, we reach further polarization in our society.

Confirmation Bias

We are bombarded with information on a daily basis. Since there is limited time in the day and so much information, we tend to limit ourselves to headlines. Snippets of information instead of the whole story. Our brains very quickly "build" the rest of the story. Except that, at that point, we stop distinguishing between facts and our own beliefs. *Confirmation bias* occurs from the direct influence of desire over beliefs. When people would like a certain idea/concept to be true, they end up believing it to be true. They are motivated by wishful thinking. This error leads the individual to stop gathering information when the evidence gathered so far confirms the views (prejudices) he or she would like to be true.[38]

Wishful thinking and confirmation bias are self-deception behaviors that can act like a drug, numbing us from the harsh reality, or forcing us to turn a blind eye toward the challenging work of collecting evidence and then thinking about it. We believe what we want to believe, and we seek confirmation to support it while ignoring information that disconfirms it.

Think of the sources of information that different people use. Democrats tend to listen and watch the NBC and CNN networks, while Republicans tend to listen and watch the FOX network. Why? Because for the most part, we like listening to other people who confirm our beliefs. Try the following exercise: whenever an important event with political consequences takes place—switch between the CNN and FOX News channels to hear the coverage. It would feel as if you are hearing about two completely different events. This media bias has sparked the ever-growing use of the term "Fake News," that started during the 2016 Presidential election. Vanessa Otero, in her blog *All Generalizations are False*, developed and maintained a map of all media outlets, their credibility (from containing inaccurate and fabricated information to original fact reporting), and their partisan bias (from conservative to liberal). It is worth looking at.[39]

Want to try something else to see how confirmation bias works? Just post something on Facebook on one of the following topics: gun control, Planned Parenthood, or school choice. Observe the discourse. Is it a discourse that includes listening? Willingness to change your mind? Or does it include confirmation bias, personal attacks, and entrenching in polarized positions?

The Demise of Corporate Innovation

The book *Culture starts with YOU, not your boss!* describes a model for creative, effective, and productive teamwork. The following is based, for the most part, on that model.

Constructive Conflict

The ability to conduct effective, productive, and creative teamwork depends first and foremost on the ability to conduct *constructive conflict*. Holding a politically correct debate is equivalent to not having a true topical debate at all. There is the "meeting *before* the meeting," and the "meeting after the meeting," just not the meeting *during* the meeting. Real issues are not discussed. They are off the table. Emotions and passion are kept in check, and holding a "civilized" meeting, in which nobody gets offended, becomes more important than holding a productive and effective meeting.

When someone's feelings are hurt because P.C. has raised their belt (sensitivity), then ideas that should have been appropriate, all of a sudden, contribute to someone feeling offended. At that point, political correctness gives way to *destructive conflict*. At that point, everything becomes personal and emotional. All of the hits are below the belt. It's not that your *idea* is stupid—*you* are stupid! Needless to say that such a conflict is neither productive nor creative.

The only way to conduct a constructive conflict is if *trust* exists among team members. The foundation for trust is shared values, perceived competence, and fairness.[40] In the presence of political correctness, shared values will exist only if everyone in the meeting is within the same in-group and think alike. However, this will also reduce the diversity of the team, which will have an adverse effect on creativity. If the members of the team are not within the same in-group, they will likely not share values, thus preventing trust from occurring among them. Being in the out-group will also affect the perception of competence of other team members. Finally, actions of members of your in-group will be considered by you to be fair, whereas the same actions taken by members of the out-group will not. In a politically correct culture, all three foundational elements of building trust (perceived competence, shared values, and fairness) are far from optimal.

Beyond the foundational-structural elements, trust in a team develops over time and is closely related to the sum of all interactions between members of the team, the amount of time they spent together, accelerated (or slowed) by the intensity of the interactions and the positivity of them.

The more political correctness you have in a team, the less time members will spend together. The interactions will be much less intense, as members would prefer phone calls over face-to-face meetings or, better yet, e-mails. The interactions will be less positive, as well. As a result, trust will take a very long time to develop, if it ever will.

And where trust doesn't exist, team members are unwilling to be vulnerable with one another enough to ask stupid questions, are not comfortable enough to offer each other constructive feedback, and are not confident enough to be receptive to such criticism. With all those factors at play—how do you expect teamwork to be productive, constructive, or creative?

Nobody ever got fired for choosing IBM

Another consequence of political correctness going too far is the fear of trying new things. In a politically correct environment, you will not hear the real feedback about what you attempted. Following the "party line" is more valued than trying counter-intuitive things. After all, "nobody ever got fired for choosing IBM."[41] When employees don't try new things, the level of innovation from an organization drops dramatically.

The Merriam-Webster dictionary defines *heuristic thinking* as:

> [I]nvolving or serving as an aid to learning, discovery, or problem-solving by experimental and especially trial-and-error methods.

> *Also:* of or relating to exploratory problem-solving techniques that utilize self-educating techniques (such as the evaluation of feedback) to improve performance.[42]

What if the student was in such a politically correct environment where someone asked a genuinely curious question as a way to better understand a concept, a historical fact, a religion, or a culture, but was met with the "how dare you ask that?!" response either verbally or non-verbally by a teacher or classmates? Would students ever want to venture forth with another question? Very unlikely. Could another possible consequence be that they decided to form their own bias and only look for information that coincided with what they had already learned? What if because they were afraid to ask questions that they decided to just "go along to get along" and participate in groupthink, confirmation bias, or incestuous amplification?

We learn through trial-and-error; any successful entrepreneur became successful only after making some mistakes along the way, but the key is that they were *allowed* to make those mistakes. The best athletes learned through trial-and-error; they had to endure the discomfort in order to train their muscles and mindset to win. One concern with political correctness and trying to make everything equal is that there may be a risk of limiting people's ability to learn heuristically. Is it not through questioning that we can learn the most? If we do not question the status quo, then how do we grow? If the only feedback that is given is, "you can't ask that, it's offensive," then who gets to decide what is offensive versus just uncomfortable to talk about because it brings our biases or lack of knowledge out into the open to be challenged?

Policies before values

The book *Conscious Capitalism*[43] proposes putting values first. However, as the Home Depot story shows, employees can get punished for doing the right thing. "What's good and what's right supersedes what's policy and what's orders," believed the employee,[44] even though he got fired for that belief. What do you do when you believe the right thing to do is not what company policy says? In a culture fraught with political correctness, following policy is more important than doing the right thing.

Employee protection

In a company that embraces political correctness, you keep unproductive employees because you simply can't get rid of them. With corrective action and diversity, as part of the overall politically correct culture, if the employee is a member of a minority group or a protected class (race, gender, age, veteran, disable, etc.), the burden of proof for low performance is extremely high. With so many protected classes, pretty much only white men can be fired relatively easily. And even then, to prevent employment-related lawsuits, you are probably better off eliminating the position than specifically the person, even if the employees were severely underperforming, or worse.

Is that protection good for employees? Not necessarily. There are many reasons why you decide not to hire someone. Race, age, gender, disability or the like cannot be viable reasons, nor should they be. But fear of the consequences of firing such an employee might be strong enough to avoid hiring them. How hard is it to find another reason? It will be very hard to prove that you didn't hire this specific individual because of any one of the forbidden reasons.

It is easier to let employees go during a reduction in force (layoffs) when you eliminate *positions* rather than employees. Even then, as an employer, you are under strict requirements to make sure the diversity among the employees you let go is proportional.

It used to be a common practice, before hiring a new employee, to check references. However, candidates would tend to provide only positive references, i.e., people who will only say good things about them. This occurs to the extent that you cannot rely on references that employees provide anymore. However, calling their previous employers is not much better. Once an employee is let go, your human resources department will instruct you to refrain from providing any negative reference, fearing lawsuits by the former employee. You would only be allowed to provide the time in which the employee worked in the company and their position. Nothing else. As a result, underperforming employees would continue to move from one employer to the next, without the need to improve. And no—it's not good for the employee, either.

Political Polarization

Another outcome of the polarization in our culture is the political polarization and partisanship. The *Massachusetts Institute for Technology* (MIT) conducted a study of the agreement and disagreement among the different parties in the 1949 to 2011 period. While there were different metrics that could be used to demonstrate that growing partisanship, the researchers chose the agreement (or disagreement) between the parties during roll-call votes in the U.S. Congress, specifically, the House of Representatives. The data was taken from the Office of the Clerk of the U.S. House of Representatives.[45]

The results were staggering. The following figure[46] shows the overlap (agreement) among the parties. It is visually easy to observe that while there was some disagreement between the parties in the 81st Congress (1949), the level of agreement increased over time, until 1969 (the 91st Congress). After that, the level of agreement consistently declines until the last data point in that research, the 112th Congress (2011), where there is almost no overlap between the parties. You could simply say that the two parties exhibit extreme partisan and polarized politics.

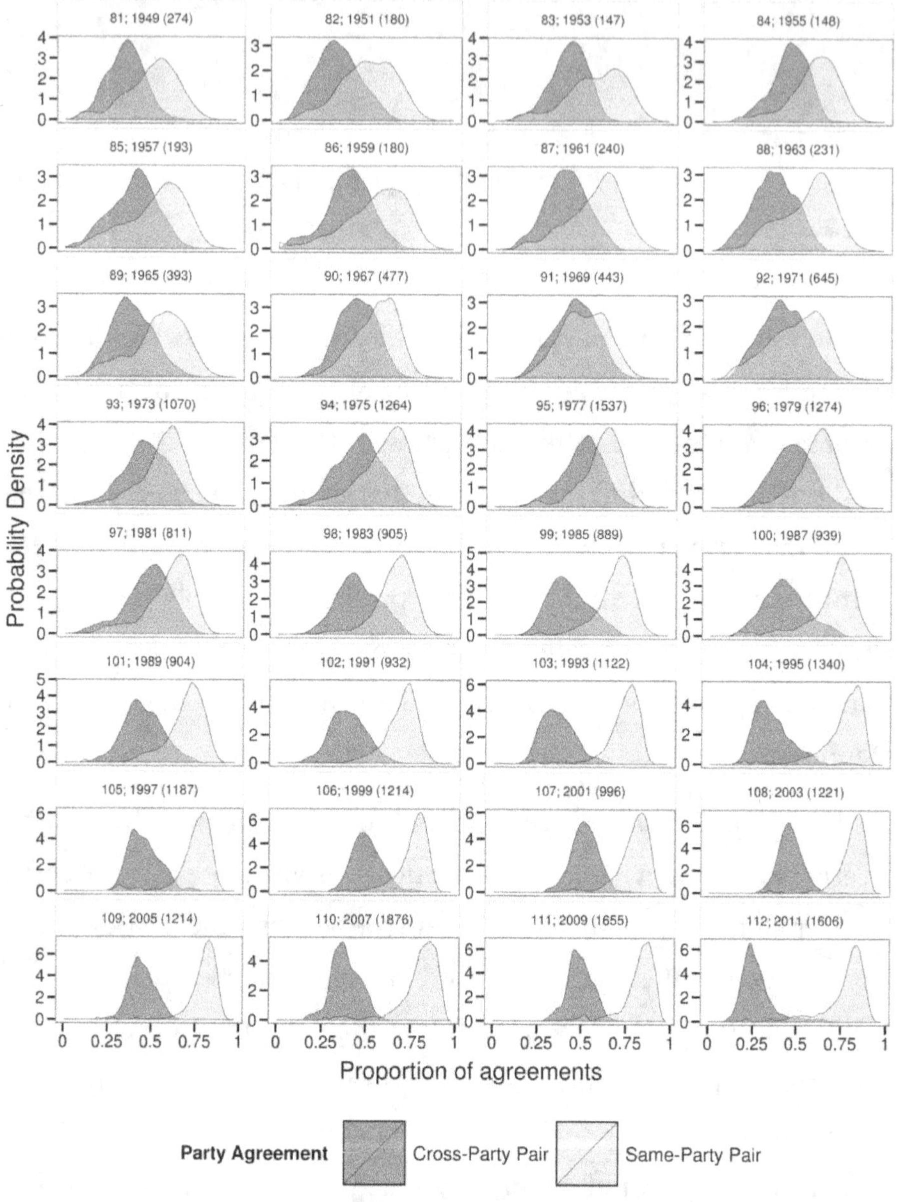

Figure 15: Political polarization

Description of the chart above from the MIT paper:

Probability density functions of same-party and cross-party pairs over time. Probability density functions of the number of roll call vote agreements between pairs of the same-party (SP) and those pairs of cross-party (CP) pairs. The plots show the steady divergence of CPs and SP agreement rates over time. Above each distribution is the Congress number (81–112), followed by the year the Congress commenced, and the number of total roll call votes during the two sessions of each Congress. Pairs with few agreements (below the local minima of a consistently- increasing CP distribution), including representatives from Washington D.C., Puerto Rico are removed.[47]

Another way to analyze the MIT findings is to compare the number of *agreements* in roll-call votes, as shown in the following chart. You can see that the two highest vote "agreements" were in 1973 (12,921) and 1969 (12,672). After that time, the numbers dramatically decline. A two-period rolling average trend line (dashed) shows that.

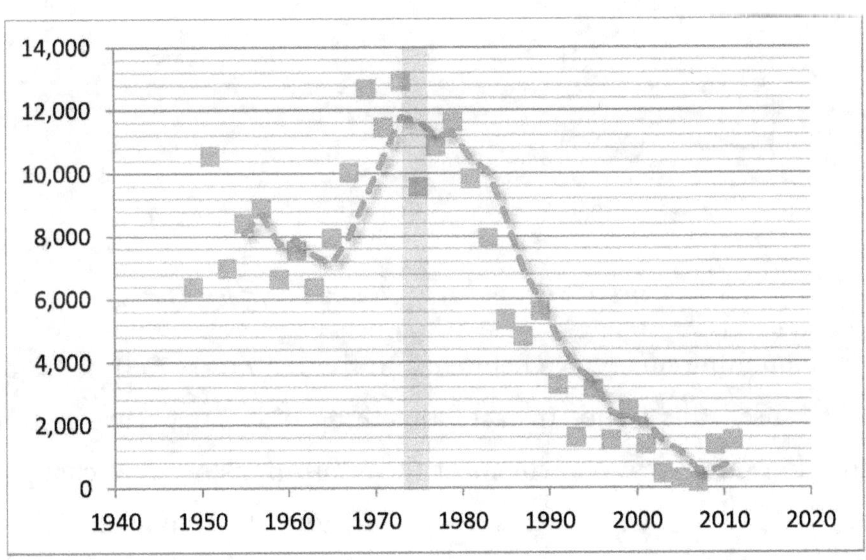

Figure 16: Cross-party agreement levels

Congress never returned to the agreement levels of 1973 or 1969.

The next way to view the data is to look at the level of *disagreement* between the parties, as shown in the following chart. The number of disagreements among parties continuously increases. However, you can see a significant jump between 1969 and 1973.

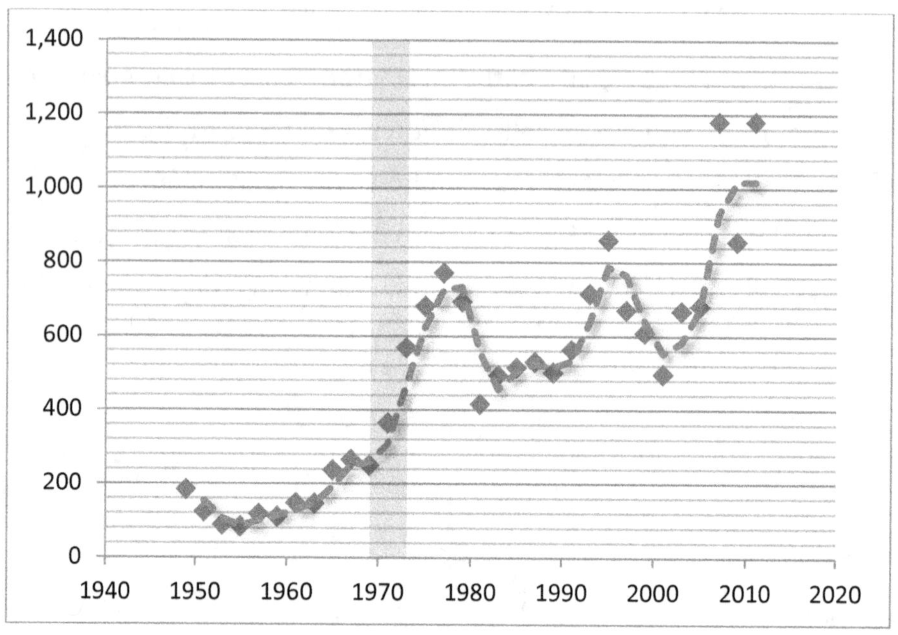

Figure 17: Cross-party disagreement levels

Something must have happened in the 1969 to 1973 time frame that caused this trend. In fact, something did. But we are getting ahead of ourselves. We will cover the event in history that changed our culture in Part 2 of this book. For now, the important fact is that the level of cross-party disagreement continued to climb.

***

How does political correctness cause political polarization? In the 2016 PEW Research we previously mentioned, you could see differences among different demographic groups with respect to the options "People need to be more careful with language to avoid offending people" versus "Too many people are easily offended these days over language." The total response indicated that 59% were in agreement with the second statement (too much political correctness), and 39% were in agreement with the first statement (we need *more* political correctness). However, when you compare the different demographic groups, you see dramatic differences.

- 78% of Republicans thought there is too much political correctness, compared to only 37% of Democrats (41% difference);
- 83% of Trump supporters in the 2016 elections thought we have too much political correctness, compared to only 39% of Clinton supporters (44% difference);
- 67% of white participants thought we have too much political correctness compared to 30% of black participants (37% difference). Hispanic participants were actually the most balanced group in its attitude towards political correctness (47% thought we had too much of it, while 49% thought we should have more);
- Finally, the difference between men and women was smaller, but still worth mentioning: 68% of men thought we have too much political correctness compared to 51% of women (17% difference); *and*
- Oddly enough, the differences across race and gender lines are larger among Democrats than among Republicans.

The *FOX News* 2017 Poll,[48] while still showing differences in percentages, demonstrated similarity in the majority attitude toward political correctness. Stating that political correctness has gone too far in this country were—

☐   66% of all participants;

☐   67% of men, 66% of women;

☐   68% of white respondents, 62% of non-white;

☐   51% of Democrats, 83% of Republican; *and*

☐   52% of Liberals, 81% of Conservatives.

***

For now, let's talk about the consequences of that political polarization. When the two main parties cannot agree on almost anything, there is a deadlock in legislation. A smaller number of bills become laws, and when they do, they typically represent a single, extreme ideological position held by the party in the majority. When Democrats have the majority of the House, Senate, and White House, new laws include the Democrat, liberal ideology. When the Republicans have the majority of the three houses, new laws include the Republican, conservative ideology. When there is no majority in either house and they are split, it is difficult to pass any legislation and the President often vetoes bills presented by a Congress of the other party.

During the 80th Congress (1947-1948), 7,611 bills were introduced in the House of Representatives, of which 1,739 (22.8%) passed. At the same time, 3,186 bills were introduced at the Senate, of which 1,670 (52.4%) passed. In the 114th Congress (2015-2016), 6,634 bills were introduced at the House, of which 896 (13.5%) passed, and of the 3,589 bills introduced in the Senate, only 427 (11.9%) passed.[49] The number of bills introduced in Congress was consistent throughout the sessions over that 65-year period, but you can see there was a dramatic decline in the number of those who actually passed and became law.

Another unfortunate outcome of this polarization and dynamic is the erosion of the trust that the public has in its government.

PEW Research[50] conducted a longitudinal study of people's trust in the government from 1958 to 2015. The results of this study were reported in 2015. They are alarming.

In 1964, the public had the most trust in the government. As many as 77% of participants then indicated that they trusted the federal government to do what is right just about always, or most of the time. That number declined significantly toward one of the lowest levels, 19% in 2015.

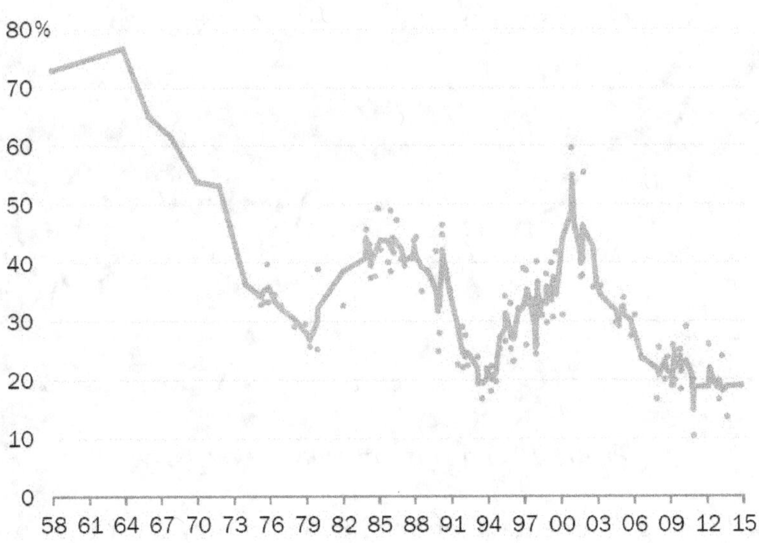

Figure 18: Public trust in government

Note that the biggest drop in public trust in the government happened within one decade—the decade that included the Vietnam War, Watergate, and civil unrest. That trust dropped from 77% in 1964 down to 36% in 1973. By 1979, only one in four Americans trusted the federal government. We will return to the impact of those events during that decade later in this book.

Not surprisingly, the numbers vary by party, depending on what party the President represented. When a Republican President was in the White House, Republicans trusted the government more than Democrats, and when a Democrat President was in the White House, Democrats trusted the government more than Republicans. However, the differences between the levels of trust across parties were less than 20%, and typically less than 10%.

Trust in government by party: 1958-2015

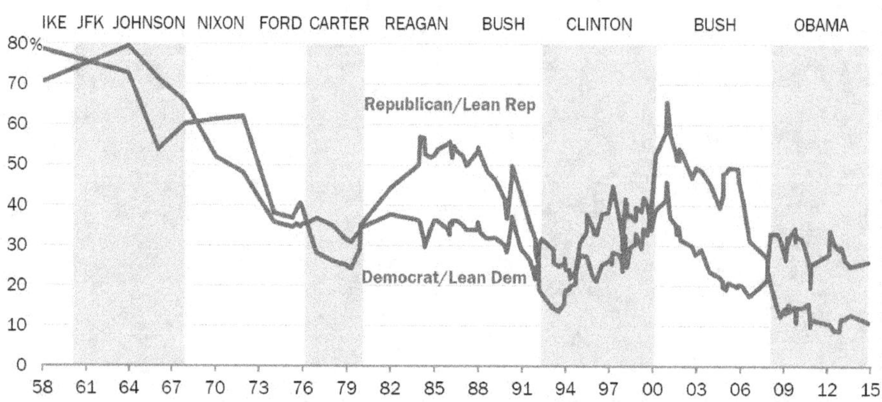

Figure 19: Trust in government by party

The average percentage of people saying they trust the government during the George W. Bush Presidency was 47% Republicans and 28% Democrats (19% difference), while the average during the Barack H. Obama Presidency was 29% Democrats and 13% Republicans (16% difference). The overall erosion of public trust in the government crossed party lines.

To make things worse, 74% of the survey respondents in 2015 believed that most elected officials put their own interests ahead of the country's and 55% of respondents believed that "ordinary Americans" would do a better job solving problems than the officials they elected into office.

Two of the best examples of the political polarization of our time are the passage of two of the most important legislative efforts in recent years: the *Affordable Care Act* ("Obamacare") and the *Tax Reform* of 2017. Obamacare was passed in the Senate in March 2010 by a party-line[51] majority of 58 Democrat, 2 independent senators, and not a single Republican senator. It then passed in the House of Representatives by a party-line majority of 219 Democrat representatives and not a single Republican. Republicans complained that the authoring and modifications of the bill, which had 2,300 pages, was done by Democrats behind closed doors.

Seven years later, a Republican legislature passed the *2017 Tax Reform Bill*. It passed the House along party lines, with 227 Republican representatives and not a single Democrat representative voting for it, and passed the Senate with 51 Republican senators and not a single Democrat senator supporting it. The complaint from Democrats? The bill had 479 pages and was developed and modified by Republicans behind closed doors. Sound familiar?

The consequences of this political polarization in Congress are legislative gridlocks, the passage of very polarized laws that align only with the majority party, and the continuous erosion of public trust in the government. Why do they do that? Because our representatives do the best they can to appeal to their support base (voters and donors), so they can be re-elected. They gave up on trying to serve all the people. Who suffers? *We, the People.*

However, the political polarization is not unique to Congress or any other branch of government. It is pervasive in our society. Once again, we turn to the PEW Research Center which, in December 2017, conducted a survey of the public's opinion on conflicts between groups in our society.[52]

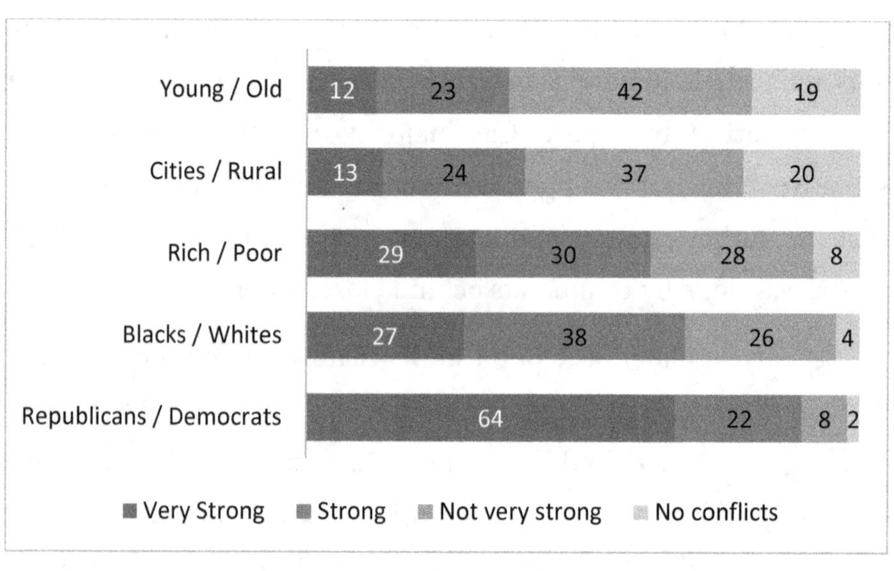

Figure 20: Conflicts between groups in society

Among the five different group categorizations, the highest level of conflict was identified by respondents as between Republicans and Democrats; 86% identified that conflict as *strong* or *very strong.*

It is the only categorization in which more than half of the respondents (64%) identified the conflict as *very strong*. It is also the categorization with the lowest number (2%) of respondents believing that there is no conflict. Our guess is that the 2% (or even the 10% who believed there is no conflict or at least not a very strong one) were simply being politically correct. But we are being facetious…

Not only that the numbers are high for political polarization, but they are also continuing to rise. In 2012, 45% of Republicans and 50% of Democrats felt that the conflict was very strong, but those numbers climbed to 65% and 66%, respectively, only five years later in 2017.

The report showed that while Democrats generally believe that there is more conflict between groups than Republicans do, the one categorization in which Democrats and Republicans agree the most (and at the highest levels of 87% and 90%, respectively) is—political polarization. To put this in simple words, the one thing that Republicans and Democrats agree on the most is that the biggest disagreements are between Republicans and Democrats. Okay, maybe not so simple words…

Researchers from USC Dornsife College of Letters, Arts, and Sciences measured the Democrat-Republican polarization through analysis of voting patterns and reached an alarming result: our country is more politically polarized today than it was during the Civil War. Using scales of 0 (neutral) to 1 (highly conservative or highly liberal), they claim that during the Civil War that distance was 0.74 (out of 2), and by 2015 it climbed to 1.08. The time in which the political preferences was the closest was between 1930 (the Great Depression) and 1977, following the Vietnam War. Throughout that entire period, the polarization was less than 0.5.[53]

Finally, in another study, PEW Research claimed that a very sizeable majority of voters (63% of Democrats and 71% of Republicans) affiliated with their party because they believed that the policies of the other party were harmful to the country. Only a few percentage points above that, they cited belonging to a party because they believe their own party had policies that were good for the country.[54]

Once again, we find that the in-group and out-group affiliations caused by political correctness are responsible for our political polarization.

P.C. in Counseling

Counseling is supposed to be non-judgmental, unbiased, and not pushing one's opinions onto the client. However, even counselors are human and make mistakes, but what about the boards, universities, and counseling associations that train and dictate the policies in which counselors must follow? Are they always unbiased, or do they err in promoting certain agendas?

One of the highest standards in counseling is that if a counselor does not feel that she or he can provide counseling that goes against his or her belief system to the point where it could potentially cause a bias or influence treatment, then the counselor is to refer the client to another counselor who does not feel any such moral, ethical, or personal conflicts. After all, why would a client want to open up to someone who may feel some type of conflict towards him or her as a person or his or her behaviors? Wouldn't a client want to see a professional who can be more neutral and/or unbiased? Given the intimate nature of the counselor-patient relationship, this would seem to make sense.

However, the *American Counseling Association*, one of the largest counseling associations in the U.S., sided with *Eastern Michigan University* (EMU) when they dismissed conservative Christian student Julea Ward because she did not feel comfortable counseling a homosexual student, as it violated her beliefs and could potentially

cause an ethical issue. Here is the description from Counseling Today, the ACA's magazine:

> The case began in 2009, when then-student Ward began her
> practicum at EMU. Upon reading the file of a client to which she
> was assigned and finding he had previously been counseled
> about his same-sex relationship, Ward, a conservative Christian,
> notified her supervisor that, in accordance with her religious be-
> liefs, she would not be able to counsel the client and needed to
> refer him to someone else.
>
> Ward's supervisor canceled the counseling session and sched-
> uled an informal review, during which EMU faculty members
> explained to Ward that she needed to abide by the university
> counseling program's policies and curricular requirements,
> which adhere to the *ACA Code of Ethics*. The *ACA Code of Eth-
> ics* states that 'counselors may not discriminate against clients on
> the basis of age, culture, disability, ethnicity, race, reli-
> gion/spirituality, gender, gender identity, sexual orientation,
> marital status/partnership, language preference, socioeconomic
> status or any basis proscribed by law.' This meant Ward was re-
> quired to set aside her personal beliefs and values when working
> with clients during practicum.[55]

Given the choice of completing a remediation program, leaving
the EMU counseling program, or requesting a formal hearing,
Ward chose the hearing. As a result of the formal hearing, she was
dismissed from the program for violating the *ACA Code of Ethics*.

Did the religious preference of the student play a role in how
this case was handled? Would the outcome be different if she were
Muslim, Hindi, Jewish, or a Satanist? Would the school and ACA
have responded the same way? We don't know the answer to that.
What if the objection was not over someone's sexual orientation, a
much politicized topic, but regarding the client's history of abor-

tion and the student had a relative who had an abortion? Often time's groups pick and choose which rules and guidelines they will follow or impose depending on their own belief systems or agendas.

The school and the ACA, in defending their stance, tried to make the student, or those who agree with her, be seen as biased, uneducated, uncaring, and/or judgmental individuals who should not be counseling if they refuse to work with certain populations. No one can walk in another person's shoes; they can attempt to try them on, but they will never truly fit. If the student or counselor has not been trained to work with a certain population, would it be ethical to send them into a room to "experiment" with a client with that issue? When supervising interns, it is clear that if they have not been trained to work with Autism, then it would be unethical to make them treat that population, especially if they had no interest in working with that group or training because their passion was in eating disorders.

While Ms. Ward initially lost by having to leave her graduate program and go through an agonizing court process, Michigan did pass SR 66, described as:

> A resolution to enact legislation protecting the rights of conscience of students seeking counseling degrees and licensed professional counselors, calls out ACA directly: 'Whereas, the American Counseling Association, a private organization that promulgates a code of ethics widely used by university counseling programs and state licensure boards in training for and regulating the counseling profession, has publicly supported universities that have punished or dismissed students for adhering to their sincere religious convictions.'[56]

But Ms. Ward's case was not the only one. Jennifer Keeton's case with Augusta State University preceded it. Keeton "claimed she was ordered to undergo remediation and alter her central religious beliefs after she revealed her religious convictions about gender identity. She filed a lawsuit against the university, which was later dismissed."[57]

There are some states that do seem to understand the logic behind not forcing counselors to go beyond their conscience, beliefs, and training. As a side note, asking a counselor to do so is tantamount to hypocrisy in the counseling room, as therapists guide patients in boundary setting, which includes the right to their opinions, feelings, religious views, morals, ethics, and to not deny them. In essence, patients are to be congruent, but counselors are not allowed to, unless they live in Michigan or Arizona.

> The Michigan House of Representatives passed House Bill 5040, or the Julea Ward Freedom of Conscience Act, that protects the right of students to object to providing certain counseling services if they conflict with the students' religious beliefs or moral convictions. This bill applies to public or private degree or certificate granting colleges, universities, junior colleges and community colleges in the state of Michigan and restricts those institutions from disciplining or discriminating against students with religious and professional conflict. Additionally, an Arizona bill was signed that protects the religious expression of students. It includes a statement that colleges of that state will not discriminate against students in counseling, social work or psychology programs because the students refuse to counsel clients about goals that conflict with the students' religious beliefs, as long as the students consult with their supervising instructors to avoid harming the clients.[58]

A Vicious Cycle

At first glance, you may question how are all of those behaviors related to political correctness? Isn't developing more laws, rules, and changes in culture and ideology supposed to help people and not hurt them? Aren't those designed to decrease bullying, discrimination, preferential treatment, and to provide to us equal treatment? Let's explore how well-meaning ideas and prosperity may have unintentionally created less resilient individuals.

Culture of convenience

Without question, the U.S. has been blessed with prosperity and modern conveniences, so that even the poor among us often have access to cell phones, food, some type of shelter, education, and, often, basic health care through free clinics. Our homeless population in the cities usually has shelters to stay in overnight and access to running water. We are not a third world country by any stretch of the imagination, but many of us have been guilty, at one time or another, of having "first world problems," i.e. complaining about things that are true luxuries in most parts of the world.

A few examples include panicking when the Internet or cell service goes down for more than five minutes, having to wait in line for a $5 cup of coffee, or kids who complain that they do not have the latest and greatest ___________ (fill in the blank). Given this prosperity, you could say that the U.S. is spoiled. Please note; this is not to say that the U.S. does not have a serious homeless population comprised of children, vets, and the mentally ill. Every night there are kids who sleep in cars, hotel rooms, or shelters with their parent(s), and in a land that is so prosperous, it seems difficult to believe that this is taking place on a daily basis all across America. There are hard working families who are struggling to get by and must make difficult decisions about what they can afford to buy at the grocery store.

Previous generations would call most Americans "soft" and without a backbone. With most jobs taking place at an office, home, school, or medical setting, the days where the large majority of the workforce worked outside in the elements of nature with their bare hands are gone. Each year, there is a decrease in the number of farms and farmers in the U.S.[59]

More recent generations may scoff at the idea of having a job where they may get dirty and very little electronic technology is used. According to the Bureau of Labor Statistics' October 2017 report, 92.9% of American jobs are non-agriculture in nature and there has been a decrease in the number of construction and manufacturing jobs in the last ten years.[60]

Often these groups, who have been the builders and suppliers for this country, feel forgotten or disenfranchised. It would be curious to examine how these groups who earn their income through the use of their hands may view some of the issues that are brought up in political correctness debates. Would they feel that their needs or concerns get equal treatment? Where are the ribbons and parades for their issues?

Some have said that we live in a "disposable" world, with the philosophy that if it is broke, throw it away and get a new one. For many, instead of learning how to fix something, it is easier to not only buy a replacement, but to get the newest version of it. Many manufacturers use cheaper parts to play into the "break and replace" Western society mindset. This is a much different mindset than previous generations, such as those who lived through the Great Depression or World War II, where families practiced re-using an item multiple times and in as many ways as possible. If something broke, then they learned how to fix it. Items were better built with higher quality materials, so they lasted longer; think about how cars or refrigerators used to be made.

In addition, there seemed to be greater appreciation for the things that we purchased; the concept of passing the furniture, car, or piece of jewelry from one generation to another was used as a selling point to denote the level of quality involved in the product. With the onset of mass production, items became cheaper to produce and quality was compromised. The increase of income in many American households and the increased pace of life, as cities grew and suburbs developed, may have planted the seeds of convenience over quality.

***

Increased convenience may have contributed to decreased patience, appreciation, and the desire to learn a new skill. When you don't have to work for something and when things come too easy, then sometimes you take them for granted. This could be a starting point for "snowflake" development. At its worst, it leads to feelings of entitlement: "I am entitled to have that shiny new object even though I did not put the work into earning it. Once I have it, I will use it up and demand that I be given a new one because it isn't fair that you have something that I want. And if you tell me that I can't have it, then I will throw a fit about it until I get what I want."

Many conveniences are literally at our finger tips with minimal effort needed to get food, change the TV channel, watch a movie, or keep up with our items (key notifications and car assistance programs tell us where we left our keys, where we parked, and help to unlock our cars). Car technology is evolving to where we do not even have to pay as much attention when we drive because our cars will apply the brakes and Parallel Park for us. As we write this book, completely autonomous cars are beginning to drive on our roads.

A final "convenience" is that the U.S. has not enacted selective service (draft) in over 40 years. Being drafted was likely never convenient for anyone; it disrupted their entire lives.

How are you expected to build endurance, perseverance, mental and physical stamina when so many challenges have been greatly decreased or eliminated from daily life? When faced with inconveniences, such as a flat tire, a cell phone that won't work, the satellite TV malfunctioning for a day, having to wait more than fifteen minutes for anything, a minor illness, or not getting a job that they feel that they deserved, how will those individuals handle these situations? What happens when there are more challenging, longer lasting situations, such as a chronic illness, divorce, death of a loved one, being too broke to buy something that they really need, such as heat on a cold day, food, or a running car?

Endurance is related to stamina, and it builds perseverance when you stick with a less-than-pleasant situation instead of running from it. You persevere during the storm, and with each storm you go through, you build a higher level of stamina physically, but also mentally, which assists with your mindset. Each passage creates a foundation of strength, endurance, and knowledge; it is cumulative and, hopefully aids in the survival of the next storm.

To use another analogy, think of skiing. Most people do not go head long onto a double black diamond slope their first day of ski school; they start off on a calm, flat surface to gain experience with the tools that they were given. However, if individuals are not allowed to get their "ski legs" on the bunny slopes of life because their caregivers or society did not want to see them fall down, then what will happen when that person is forced to get up on that ski lift to go to bigger slopes? Sometimes the "school of hard knocks" is the best teacher, but what if parents, schools, and the government intervenes where the child isn't exposed to those learning and growth opportunities? That is another factor that may contribute to the development of "snowflakes."

The snowflake effect

The term "snowflake" is typically used in a condescending way to describe any person who seems to "melt under the pressures of life." The *Urban Dictionary* states that a snowflake is:

> A very sensitive person. Someone who is easily hurt or offended by the statements or actions of others. [An important item to note is that] this has nothing to do with politics. Snowflakes can be liberal or conservative. Whether it is a compliment or an insult is a matter of opinion and depends on the context.[61]

For some who fall under this category, they may be at risk for going through another round of being a toddler, or what could be referred to as "toddlerdom;" this is exhibited by increased sensitivity to any comment that they may not agree with, the sense that their opinion and feelings may be overly important, as evidenced through the many videos, blogs, and posts. Their patience level is being measured in seconds, not hours. The lack of patience could contribute to emotionally-based decisions instead of well-thought out, logical decisions with the potential result of a short term benefits focus instead of the long term consequences of each decision. In deciding rules, policies, and laws, this mindset is dangerous, as laws that may benefit those today may end up costing people or society a few decades later.

We assume that anyone who willingly decides to become a parent will have the best interest for his or her child in mind; they have decided to equip themselves with training or knowledge they received from healthy role modeling. Caregivers are to look out for possible risks of physical or emotional hazards and intervene. But where and when does a parent draw the line before protection becomes potential enabling? When does helping become possible hurting? What are the implications of being "too protective" of our children?

Whether we wish to admit to it or not, our parenting style is influenced by how we were parented, and in times of stress with a child, we are likely to "go with what we know" and act upon the role modeled parenting lessons of our parents. Some caregivers may choose to go in the exact opposite direction of their parents and not replicate any lessons or behaviors. This can be seen when a parent who was physically abused by their parent decides to never lay a hand on the child, not even a pop on their butt when they misbehave. Another example is a parent who felt that their parents were "too strict" and decides to have more of a "permissive" or laissez faire approach with their child with very little boundaries, rules, or consequences.

How does this relate to P.C.?

First, let's answer the aforementioned questions. When caregivers do not know where to "draw the line" between what is permissible versus restricted, the child invariably suffers with the lack of consistent boundaries and consequences. As the child grows, if the child does not have a clear sense of right and wrong, private versus shared, or has experienced inconsistent consequences, then they may grow to be a confused individual with some anxiety; the confusion stems from the fact that they do not have a clear sense of self or what society expects of them. Humans desire structure and consistency, which can take place in the form of rules.

> Rules aren't all good. Bad ones create 'customs… in complete
> opposition to the true welfare …of mankind,' wrote Darwin:
> Even an absurd rule or belief 'constantly inculcat-
> ed…early…appears to acquire almost the nature of an instinct…
> [which is often]…followed independently of reason.'[62]

One concern is that these individuals may be easily influenced by other, more dominant or persuasive individuals. Being easily persuaded can create "followers" of an ideology without perhaps challenging the tenets of it.

> Followers don't care what their thinking strategies or general
> disposition is. They do not feel the need to acquire the
> knowledge about nurturing intelligence. They react to situations
> in their environment by spontaneous reaction, without applying
> critical thinking and without analyzing their position. They
> would more often indulge in gossip, rather than meaningful ex-
> change of ideas on challenging topics. They have less tolerance
> for views of others which are divergent from their own.[63]

There have been several cases where crowd goers are asked why are they at that rally or stand for that cause, and some do not really understand the cause or back-story of the event. They may spit out a slogan or a headline, but when pushed a bit farther—there are blank looks, irritability, or the repetition of another phrase or slogan. Sadly, not everyone who attends a rally or supports a cause really understands what the event is truly about; they are just following along with the crowd.

Are you starting to see how these items can connect with a P.C. mindset where those in authority have to tell people how to think and behave? It is easier for them just to "follow" and not ask questions. Sadly, there are times where it may look like the "blind leading the blind" in determining what is "correct."

Another unintended consequence of not knowing where to draw the line is that the child/teen may become enabled if they are not allowed to experience disappointment, hurt, frustration, sadness, grief, etc. If the parent "rescues" them out of any uncomfortable, challenging, frustrating, sad, anxiety-provoking event, then when does the child learn how to cope with those events? From where and when will they develop their coping skills? Is it the parent's intent to continue to protect or rescue their child into adulthood?

> Today's generation of young people has not developed some of the life skills kids did 30 years ago because adults swoop in and take care of problems for them. When we rescue too quickly and over-indulge our children with 'assistance,' we remove the need for them to navigate hardships and solve problems on their own. It's parenting for the short-term and it sorely misses the point of leadership—to equip our young people to do it without help.[64]

While we do see cases of parents still rescuing their adult child from things like criminal charges or financial irresponsibility, many parents start to realize when the child is in high school or college, that they cannot continue to "bail them out" of problems. However, teens or young adults may demand that the parents take care of their problems that they created because the parents had done it for decades. Some teens would say that their parents owe it to them because it was the parents' fault for enabling and teaching them to wait until someone else took care of their mess; they never had to experience disappointment and now they do not know what to do with that feeling. A few may say that because they have always been protected and helped out of situations that they are now "entitled" to continue to have the same treatment from everyone, that no one should treat them any differently than how their caregivers treated them until now. We think of people being entitled due to their position or circumstances in life, but we sometimes miss the fact that entitlement is taught (a.k.a. spoiled) and that the teen with entitlement issues is one day soon going to get a rude awakening that the rest of the world does not care about how they think that they should be treated. Businesses have rules and consequences, and an entitled attitude from an employee will lead to no work peer connections and a potential firing if customers complain.

Is it possible that a teen or young adult who has had minimal exposure to unpleasant or upsetting events can become so overwhelmed with an event or series of events that they become depressed, anxious, overwhelmed, hopeless, etc. because they do not know what steps to take in responding to it? They have not had to work through those feelings to find healthy ways to resolve the hurt and/or how to frame it as a learning experience.

> Even just looking at the confidence factor. What are parents really saying when they rescue the teen from consequences or 'life'? It can feel like a vote of no confidence. The parent is, in effect, telling the teenager: 'I don't think you can handle this, so I am going to handle it for you,'[65]

While each generation has its own unique stressors and challenges, throughout the decades, some stressors remained the same. Students in every generation have experienced social and academic concerns, been worried about the state of their families, and/or financial issues. Sadly, each generation had those who drank or popped pills as a way to deal with stress, while others may have fallen into the false sense of control with self-injury, eating disorders, and perfectionism. Research indicates that the percentage of students who use these unhealthy coping mechanisms is higher now than in any previous generation. We know that there is more of a wide spread problem with substance abuse, self-injury, and suicide than in decades past. While there are parents who model these behaviors, it would be a mistake to blame them solely for the actions of their teens.

So if the problems are essentially the same, then why did "snowflakes" or "cupcakes" emerge? Has our level of resiliency changed? Or is it that our exposure to smaller level events has been compromised, so that a foundation for coping with life was not properly laid?

> Beginning in the 1980s, American childhood changed. For a variety of reasons—including shifts in parenting norms, new academic expectations, increased regulation, technological advances, and especially a heightened fear of abduction (missing kids on milk cartons made it feel as if this exceedingly rare crime was rampant)—children largely lost the experience of having large swaths of unsupervised time to play, explore, and resolve conflicts on their own. This has left them more fragile, more easily offended, and more reliant on others.[66]

Each time a child or teen was "rescued" from a consequence that they should have received, could that instead be one more layer of exposure that would help him or her to build more resiliency? Ideally, with each situation, the parents sit down and explain the event in language the child understands. However, when parents shield their kids from the age-appropriate realities of life, they risk unintentionally harming the child for when a bigger event comes, and there is nothing the parents can do to shield them from the realities of it. The concern is that the teen or young adult becomes overwhelmed because their brain does not know how to process it, as there are no previous experiences to draw upon.

In a conversation with a college peer, discussing a fellow student who had not lost any grandparents, not endured divorce, or other known significant life events, was revealing. He said that he did not envy her because she was now an adult, had not developed those coping skills or resiliency, and that when "life happens" that she will be more devastated by it than the rest of us who had experienced deaths, bullying, divorces, etc.

Enabling leads to entitlement

As teens become young adults, they may start to demand that special accommodations be made when they aren't needed. Students may try to make a case to their parents or teachers as to why they can't be expected to keep up with the course work in their classes, even though they signed up for that class of their own volition. The parents may then intercede on the student's behalf and complain to the teacher or coach instead of letting it be a learning experience for the student; the situation would allow them to approach the teacher with the concerns or take ownership that they signed up for that class or extracurricular activity.

At home, the child or teen may complain that they do not have time to do the basic chores of keeping their room and bathroom clean, much less help out with the dishes or vacuum once a week. However, the minor does seem to have plenty of time to keep up with their social media or video games. The parent gives in because it is "just easier to do it themselves" instead of getting into a battle. So, what lesson do you think the child just learned from those interactions? Could it be that if I just avoid, whine, pout, get emotional, etc. that I will eventually get out of my responsibilities?

As time progresses and they move into the work world, they may want to push for lower standards, less challenging work, more holidays, but still the same pay. If the boss doesn't agree, then the group may find a way to shame the boss or the company until they give into the demands to stop the unwarranted, bad publicity. A few months later, there might be a new cause to protest, and the threats and demands roll back out. The new accommodations cost the company money and employees have to be let go. And the reason? Because their parents were overly protective or politically correct with them and shielded them from the realities of life.

The "entitlement" issue is also demonstrated by newly graduated master level counselors. Many of them do not have a license, but expect to be financially compensated as if they were fully licensed. The concept of "paying your dues" is foreign to many in recent generations. Some oddly believe that they know all that they need to know from graduate school, so what could a seasoned counselor possibly be able to tell them? Hiring or keeping an employee with that attitude could be a costly mistake for your practice.

While many of these behaviors and misguided philosophies are done out of good intentions, the consequences are negative. Overprotection is actually more harmful than preservation. They may be like an exposed nerve that reacts negatively to even the smallest breeze of an issue or a snowflake that easily melts under the slightest pressure.

And what happens when teens believe that they are invincible and can do anything? Two 16 year old North Texas teens were killed and one was seriously injured in a car crash when one of the teens drove a 2016 *Porsche Macan* at a very high speed into a tree and caught fire.[67] As a side note, Texas laws prohibit a driver under the age of 18 from driving a car with more than one passenger in the vehicle under the age of 21 who is not a family member.[68] Yet, there were three unrelated teens in a high-performance car, driving significantly over the speed limit.

The consequences of entitlement went even beyond that in 2013. On June 15, 16-year old Ethan Couch drove his Ford F-350 pick-up truck under the influence of alcohol and Valium (drinking age is 21). Driving at speeds of nearly 70 miles per hour, he lost control over his truck and hit a stalled vehicle on the side of the road, hitting and killing four, and injuring seven teens riding in his car, one of which remains paralyzed.[69] We should note that the F-350 can carry only six passengers, including the driver, and remind you that a 16-year-old probationary driver can only have one passenger under the age of 21 who is not a family member in the car. Couch was charged with four counts of intoxication manslaughter and two counts of intoxication assault. He admitted his guilt. However, during the sentencing hearing, the powerhouse legal team hired by Couch's parents called psychologist Dick Miller, who testified that Couch's wealthy upbringing and a lack of consequences for his actions earlier in life caused him to "suffer" from "affluenza." This defense was successful, and Ethan Couch was sentenced to two years of probation, instead of the 20-year prison sentence that the prosecutors sought.

Following the criminal case, the families of those killed or hurt in the crash filed civil lawsuits, all of which were settled.

At this point, you would expect that he would have learned his lesson and show remorse. However, he was seen drinking at a party in violation of his probation conditions, and then fled to Mexico with his mother. He was eventually caught and brought back to the U.S., where he served two years in prison for violating the conditions of his probation,[70] not for killing four and injuring seven more.

At the time of writing of this book, Ethan Couch was expected to be released from jail soon.[71]

Schools

How do schools contribute to snowflake building? They have rules and consequences that they fairly consistently follow, so how could there be boundary issues with an academic institution?

Some schools could be seen as "the land of second chances" when it comes to test re-takes and being able to turn in homework days up to weeks after it was due. One reason for this is that public schools feel the pressure to keep their *Blue Ribbon* or *Exemplary* status, even to the detriment of the students that they keep passing along from one grade to the next, as in the case with several students encountered in therapy and in the college classroom.

One of the most egregious examples of schools enabling students was the case of a Texas school teacher who was giving the standardized test answers to students. Another reason is the expansion of the political correctness used by parents to influence the schools; this is to the detriment of the students because the schools and parents both are being overly sensitive to students' feelings, more so than preparing them for life (which, after all, is going to be somebody else's problem). The reality is that students who keep getting enabled to not learn, to not do their work in a timely manner, and to not study for the test the first time, may not learn the important life skills of time management, responsibility taking for studying and turning assignments in, and organization.

For the most part, colleges are not as lenient as public schools are in that respect. Imagine the surprise the new college freshmen will have when they learn that there are no late papers or ones without at least some stiff penalties attached to it. Is it possible that the freshman may become overwhelmed when someone shares a dissenting opinion, that the professor does not care if they overslept for the exam, or that there is no make-up test? How will the formerly shielded freshman cope? Could some of them start demanding of the faculty and administration that re-do tests be allowed? Could they even say that the questions are too difficult and not all of the students in the class understand them, therefore posing the idea that the tests be made simpler and in multiple languages?

However, more and more colleges may give into the demand to avoid bad press in a world where just about every college student is armed with a smart phone with a quick camera. What are the consequences of "giving in" instead of having dialogues with practical solutions? Is a precedent then set by the student body that if there is enough bad PR and complaining, that the school may give in? Given that fear is one of the underlying causes that keep P.C. growing, what happens if the administration starts to give in a little bit for fear of a group of students creating problems?

It has been said that one should not do anything more than once that you do not want to become a habit. Each time a group gives into the demands of another party without addressing the potential consequences (long term and short term) or negotiating the deal, the group increases the likelihood of becoming stuck in a circle of demands, fears, and enabling. Another cliché to consider would be that schools and businesses cannot be "all things to all people," that it is impossible to please every student, parent, or student group.

Participation trophies

Parents or schools who are over-protective of children and teens may be setting them up for future failures. A case in point might be participation trophies. Political correctness drives schools and organizations to offer trophies so that nobody's feelings would be hurt, especially those who have not worked hard enough to win a "real" trophy. While everyone likes to be acknowledged for their contributions, at the same time, the world is set up where there are those who win contests, jobs, or scholarships and those who do not. The inadvertent lesson of those trophies may be that no matter what your level of effort or talent, you will be rewarded for it. Life simply does not work that way. There are no participation trophies at the Olympics, for college scholarships, or at work.

There are potentially negative consequences of these trophies:

> Studies have shown that rewarding kids just for participating can have a negative impact, producing a self-obsessed, irresponsible, and unmotivated generation of false achievers. At the far end of the spectrum, inflated self-esteem has been found in criminals, junkies, and bullies, which is supposed to have been what the self-esteem movement was trying to steer children away from.[72]

Just because you graduated from high school does not mean that you will automatically be granted admission into an Ivy League university. In the workplace, a candidate may have a college degree, but if it isn't tailored to that job's specific needs or the candidate did not grow their professional skills the same way another candidate did, then the company on Madison Avenue is under no obligation to give the less qualified candidate a "participation" job.

Who doesn't like receiving some type of recognition, praise, or a shiny object to place upon a shelf? However, does the award mean the same thing if you did nothing of merit to earn it? Would you say that it is a hollow victory? Would you cherish it as much as the award for which you put more time, energy, effort, and that may have really tested your skills or stamina? According to student athlete, Betty Berdan:

> Trophies used to be awarded only to winners, but are now little more than party favors: reminders of an experience, not tokens of true achievement. When awards are handed out like candy to every child who participates, they diminish in value.[73]

Isn't it the teachers or coaches that pushed us the hardest that we tend to remember their lessons more than the "blow off" class or sport? "[T]he self-esteem movement failed to teach kids how to succeed, and giving kids a participation trophy stunts their competitive edge" according to author Ashley Merryman.[74]

Where does one draw the line on giving everyone a participation trophy? If the school or group stops giving out awards at some arbitrary age, has there been some skills training given to help those who will no longer receive the awards just because they signed up for the event in order for them to understand what is needed to succeed? To stop giving a reward without education as to the new standards and ways to adjust to those standards almost seems as if the system is setting up some students to fail.

Imagine a child who has been given a "100" each day in class for just sitting in the room and not getting into trouble. That child isn't graded on their assignments. One day, after several years, the child is told that they will no longer receive the "100," but not given a reason as to why. The child reacts negatively with confusion, anger, and some self-doubt; they may act out a bit because of all of these emotions. They are ignored, but not given a consequence. After so many times, they figure out that "being bad" isn't getting them what they want, so they will try to being pleasant, but that doesn't work either. They see some students reacting the same way they did, but there are a few who are now receiving the "100." Because they still haven't figured out what those students are doing differently, they become jealous and try to pressure those students into giving them the information. The students may demand that the standards be changed. The real problem is that the rules changed and no one told them how to cope with the change.

What would happen if the teacher decided that it was easier to just give into the demands of the students who were complaining instead of trying to assist them? The teacher decides to set up two different standards—those who are doing the work will continue to be judged by the work and can earn up to a "100," and those who can't figure out what to do or feel that the standard is unfair will automatically get a "100." To have one group continue to work to earn their "100" while another group receives the same grade for much less effort seems to be a disservice and, even, an insult to both groups.

The risk by creating that discrepancy in the work load is that resentment may develop in those who truly worked for the "100" towards those who didn't work as hard, yet earned the same grade. This resentment could start manifesting itself in bullying, looking down upon those other students as being inferior, and ostracizing them. The group that did not *earn* the "100" may not only experience those consequences by their peers, but may also develop a lower sense of confidence in their ability to try new things, decrease their self-esteem, feel less worthy than their peers, create their own in-group to spend time with, and reduce their educational opportunities because of how other teachers may perceive them. And, of course, they will see those who did *earn* the grades as an out-group. So, a situation that was designed to make people feel equal actually created inequality; you cannot have two different standards in school or the workforce.

In the 1990s to early 2000s, the buzzword on college campuses was *affirmative action.* The following is taken from the *American Civil Liberties Union's* (ACLU) website:

> The ACLU Racial Justice Program actively supports affirmative action to secure racial diversity in a number of settings to help ensure equal opportunities for all people. Affirmative action is one of the most effective tools for redressing the injustices caused by our nation's historic discrimination against people of color and women, and for leveling what has long been an uneven playing field. A centuries-long legacy of racism and sexism has not been eradicated despite the gains made during the civil rights era.[75]

If you stop to think about this premise, it isn't really making the playing field even if you let some students in, not because of merit and ability, but because of their race; that seems like reverse discrimination. And if the student who is allowed to be admitted under those conditions knows that this is how they were admitted, how does that knowledge affect them? When they compare SAT scores or GPA with their freshman peers, how might that affect how their peers view them? How will it affect their own personal beliefs about their abilities or confidence? There are some who will do their best to prove everyone wrong and show that they absolutely deserve to be at that school because of their *current* performance, but there may be some who feel intimidated, doubt their abilities, and could even fall into a self-fulfilling prophecy and fail.

In an effort to create "equal" admissions, they are actually making it unequal because the admissions process is no longer a blind process based upon performance, but is now one based on your DNA. Maybe this is taking it to an extreme, but if we based admissions on appearance, then should we look into the possibility that some colleges may only let the attractive students in and not the unattractive, even if they are both qualified? We know that there are cases of that in the work place, so is it not also possible that this could take place at the collegiate level?

What about the value of the degree and what it stands for? Is the degree worth less when students who did not earn their admissions letter into the school through grades and tests, but through a physical trait? Doesn't that potentially lower the admissions' numbers for average GPA and SAT that colleges love to brag about? In a way, this is similar to a participation trophy for college. Some students did not have the grades or test scores to earn their spot, but they are now admitted, perhaps bumping out other students who did follow the rules and did the work. Maybe the solution to creating an equal admissions playing field is to remove the race/ethnicity question and any photos from the initial paperwork. Once they are admitted, then an inquiry into racial, ethnic, and other demographic information can be requested for scholarship purposes. Below are two cases where affirmative action was not about equality.

We witnessed an example of affirmative action gone wrong. Two women applied to the same law school. One had excellent scores, grades, recommendations from recognized leaders in Los Angeles, years of work experience, and just shy of a Master's degree in Education. The other candidate did not have the same recommendation letters, work experience, or a Masters' degree. She was accepted, but the more qualified applicant was not. You could surmise that the less qualified candidate was admitted due to her being younger or a member of a minority group, but either way, the Texas law school tarnished their credibility that day by lowering the bar. Now, what do you think that each candidate learned that day?

Another example we witnessed involved a mixed race student in California, who never identified himself as Hispanic on his applications or in day-to-day life. Suddenly, when he needed to get into law school and his grades were quite lacking in comparison to other candidates, he became Hispanic on his application. While it cannot be confirmed without speaking to the admissions counselors, there is a possibility that he was either admitted due to his minority status, or that he was alum of the undergraduate institution where the law school was located, but it was likely not on merit.

The U.S. Supreme Court addressed reverse discrimination in the 1978 court case of *University of California v. Bakke* stating that:

> [T]he use of race as a criterion in admissions decisions in higher education was constitutionally permissible," it ruled that racial quotas were not, and ordered the school to admit Bakke. In other words, the court said that affirmative action was okay in some contexts, but not that specific one. Today, the University of California has no affirmative action policy.[76]

The above case was in regards to medical school admissions. Would you rather have a doctor who was admitted to medical school based on his or her own merits and abilities, or a doctor who was let in for a quota based on race, gender, or any other criteria that has nothing to do with their ability as a doctor, and that may be less qualified? When your child is seriously ill, which doctor do you want?

Does affirmative action happen on the administrative level at colleges? A third instance of possible affirmative action that we personally witnessed was at a junior college in the Dallas area and it involved a full time professor position. There were two male candidates; one had been an instructor for decades in the U.S. and in Europe and had written several books. The other candidate was young, had not written any books, had not taught internationally, and had limited professional experience in the field in which he was teaching, yet, he was given the job over the more experienced candidate. While many staff members liked both candidates on a personal level, there were some negative feelings directed toward the president of the college who chose the young candidate because it was seen as being based on racial issues. The president happened to be the same background as the candidate who received the position. While there may be other factors, those professors in that division lost respect for the president that day for her pick for that position. It is also a concern for the students and what they may have potentially missed having a different professor with more varied experiences. The one who did receive the position was a good professor who cared about his students, but so was the other candidate. Job selection should be unbiased and greatly influenced by what is on the resume and not what is on the demographics sheet.

In life, you typically do not get a trophy, admission, or a position just for doing the job that you were hired to do, unless you are in a profession that merits such praise, like the military or first responders, where each day you could lose your life because you are trying to protect or help another person. By high school, awards are typically given out on merit; first, second, and third places are earned at contests, champions crowned in playoff sporting events, and class rankings established. The concept of making every student equal and not having a class ranking, due to political correctness, would risk taking away the motivation to try to do well in school.

Why not help students who are not academically gifted, for one reason or another, find other outlets where they excel instead of not celebrating the accomplishments of those who have been able to meet the rigors of school? Why take away the acknowledgment of long hours, deferred social life, and, typically, sacrificed sleep, for fear that someone's feelings might be hurt because they aren't wearing that ribbon or ranked at a certain level? What about the feelings of those who made those sacrifices, do they not count, as well? We strongly believe that each student should have equal opportunity to access the school's resources. There needs to be a focus on concrete ways to reach equality that bring people up to the same level, such as all students in a district get a notebook or laptop computer and not only the students who attend the wealthier schools. Every school in the district should offer the opportunity to attend certain cultural events or participate in field trips. The focus should be equality in *raising* the bar, not lowering it and undermining the potential of others out of political correctness.

Media, sports, and equality

We are surrounded by media influences every single day, from the TV shows we watch, the ads in papers and magazines, the pop ups on the Internet, and social media. We can spend countless hours scrolling through each day while listening to music that interjects jingles, gossip, and occasional news. Digital marketing experts estimate that most Americans are exposed to between 4,000 and 10,000 advertisements each day.[77] With this incredible power, how much influence do you think that the media has on political correctness?

Let's examine the media's impact on what initially seems like a benign, even positive promotion of kids being valuable, special, and having rights to speak up. All of those traits are true—each child has value, a gift, and has the right to state their opinion. However, what happens when these ideas are taken to the extreme? In life, the key is *balance* because when we go to extremes, we tend to make mistakes. A child has value, but one child is no more valuable than another child. Each child is special, but no child is inherently "more special" than another. Each child, and for that matter, any person, has a right to their opinion, but not to the detriment of not allowing others to state theirs. Sometimes the media "plays favorites" with whose opinions are broadcasted and who is picked as being "more interesting" to follow or listen to.

As of 2013, only 7 percent of journalists identified as Republicans, claimed Lars Wilnat and David Weaver, professors of journalism in Indiana.[78] In addition, "since 2008, the distribution of newspaper and online publishing jobs has grown less representative of the nation as a whole." There seems to be a bias against the media being located in "the heartland" that tends to have different values than the two coasts. For instance, "73 percent of all Internet publishing jobs are concentrated in either the Boston-New York-Washington-Richmond corridor or the West Coast crescent that runs from Seattle to San Diego and on to Phoenix."[79] So, how do the media influence a blank slate of a child into one that is entitled?

In a world where kids are raised with a "princess and hero culture" in movies, books, video games, TV shows, and songs, where everything they do is a praise worthy event that is posted on social media, that they are so uniquely special that comparisons that indicate otherwise should be shunned, discouraged, and possibly ignored, we have inadvertently created a false reality for these children. While the media profits and becomes defensive of anyone who would dare challenge their content, children will suffer as they are being molded into images that the media says are "good and acceptable." Should the parents actively intervene in what their children are listening, reading, and watching? Should they be engaging their children in what they are seeing and hearing to process the messages and instill their own values and set boundaries with behaviors? We believe so. However, how many parents do either? Those are easier to do when the child is young, but often times parents back off once the child becomes a teen. Thus, during some of the most impressionable and vulnerable periods of their lives and, all too often, we are letting the media instruct our children how they should act, think, and feel.

Let's go back to princess and hero worlds. The false sense of reality that because you are a "princess" or a "hero" you get special treatment and even passes on poor behavior is a view that will surely be shattered by the harsh realities of the real world; others do not care if you "don't feel like turning in your work because you had a bad day," that you have a mild headache, so you can't play in a team sport, or that you need to skip a test because you are upset over an election. The world will not stop for them and their excuses. While some schools and parents continue to coddle their "princess" or "super hero," social media posts by "trolls" will gladly inform them that they are not special and to stop being {insert expletives here}. If these attitudes are left unchecked, they can possibly lead to a superiority complex or even narcissism.

✷✷✷

Even social media plays a role in shaping our political positions and affiliations:

> 'One of the great things and one of the horrible things about social media is that everyone can have their say,' says Juana Summers, an editor for CNN Politics. 'It's kind of a marketplace for ideas. And some voices that sometimes are not correct or have a very partisan slant can oftentimes get amplified.'[80]

"The thoughts of two billion people every day are steered by 50 people in Mountain View," stated Tristan Harris, former ethics advisor for *Google*.[81]

The media has created "Reality Stars" that have made millions for their poor, spoiled, entitled behaviors that often depict disrespect to authority and bullying of others. The worse the behavior, the higher the ratings soar. What lesson does that potentially instill in young, impressionable viewers? A case in point is Danielle "Cash Me Outside How Bow Dah" Bregoli, who became famous/infamous after she was rude to Dr. Phil McGraw on his show, and now she is making millions of dollars as a minor. The more entitled someone becomes; the less likely they are to make rational, unemotional decisions. Some adapt the proverbial, "if it feels good, do it" motto for their life and encourage others to do the same, and the media feeds into it.

The original intention of political correctness aimed to create a level playing field where one group is not raised up into a superior position over another group, especially for unhealthy, unproductive behaviors. To lift a group over their competitors is only reversing the party positions of the original problem, instead of solving it. But that's not what P.C. is doing. Depending on where you live, football is king and the football players and cheerleaders sometimes receive preferential treatment, even to the point of having grades altered so that they can be eligible for competition or "being allowed" to break rules without much consequence.

Even the media plays into the preferential treatment of some sports over others. The "Friday Night Lights" concept isn't just a saying, a book, a movie, or a TV show; it is also what gets air time on every Friday night newscast. In many media outlets, and at schools, even some associated groups are raised to a certain level above others. Cheerleaders and drill team members are seen as the "popular" groups, but band members are less glorified.

When Lori was an intern in a public, North Texas school district, a group of cheerleaders attended a school dance in an intoxicated state. The school turned them away and, as punishment, told them that they could not cheer at the games and face other consequences. Instead of the parents supporting the school and reprimanding the girls who broke the law and school policy, a group of them came together and threatened the school with a lawsuit. The school backed down on the consequences, and the girls learned an important lesson: if you have parents who are litigious enablers with money, then you can make legal threats that could cost the school money and get your way. It is also an example of how schools, just like businesses, fear lawsuits and bad publicity. For the students of the school, they may see it as a lesson that, "if you're popular, then you get special treatment."

Do you think that if it were a different group of students, say choir kids or the chess team, would the outcome have been the same? It very well may have turned out the same way. You have to wonder whether it isn't also the parents of the "popular" kids who are also entitled and that is part of what they are role modeling. Think back to your own school days when you saw preferential treatment of one group over another. We would love to think that those cases do not happen in today's world of equality and fairness in schools, due to laws and policies, but contemplate this idea: which extracurricular activity brings in the most money for a school? Which group receives more attention when it comes to the school paper, pep rallies, or announcements? The economist would say that if that group, in this case football, is the "bread winner" for the school, then, by all means, they should get the new uniforms first, get more public attention, the big, $60 million dollar stadiums, higher salaries for coaches than other teachers, and "assistance" from teachers to help the athletes who keep the program going and bringing in the dollars. Saying that football players deserve special treatment (funding or attention) over other athletes or groups is raising one group above the others, but this is not a battle that many P.C. followers in the South, or probably others areas, too, are willing to fight.

However, this is where the original premise of P.C. has not entered into schools. Where is the equal treatment in girls' team sports compared to boys? Yes, male dominated sports may bring in more money, but if even half of the same attention and dollars were given to female athletes, would there be a shift in attendance and attitude? There is focus on political correctness in making tests equal and dumbing down some academic standards (re-tests, turning in assignments late), but what about the "correctness" of equality on the literal playing field? It still seems as if the powers that be got to "pick and choose" whom or what areas should be equal, and which don't have to be equal. Isn't that the most hypocritical of all of the political correctness movement? The reality is that there are inconsistencies within political correctness; people do "pick and choose" which causes are deemed worthy enough for which to fight, raise lawsuits, get media attention, or create legislation.

However, we must ask as we look at various P.C. rules, laws, and mindset to see if P.C. solved more problems than they created. The home and the school-room are two locations that influence mind-sets and practices of behaviors or ideology from a very young age. That is where we get "stuck in our little bubbles" and have a bias toward listening only to ideas that are "comfortable" and "easy" for us to accept. To accept something because the masses do or because it's the popular trend, and you want to avoid backlash or being an outcast, is irresponsible of the person who fails to learn about what it is that they are accepting. A blind following of anything without questioning the tenets of it, the thought process or motivation behind it, the impact on yourself, others, and society as a whole, and its implementation and continuance, is not only an uneducated approach, but it is also dangerous. History shows a trail of such incidents, and the outcomes have been discrimination, increased crime, financial stressors, and world wars.

And how do we "get stuck in our bubbles" and tune out other, contrasting information? Simple—through *Confirmation Bias.*

Tying it all together

Parents, teachers, counselors, and professors are talking about the growing fragility they see. It's hard to avoid the conclusion that the overprotection of children and the hypersensitivity of college students could be two sides of the same coin. By trying so hard to protect our kids, we're making them too safe to succeed.[82]

Political correctness is an ideology or thought process that has contributed to the writing of legislation at a local, state, and federal level. These acts have influenced parenting styles, the media, and academia. Often times with students, the three of these collide. However, have we created a generation of students who have been strongly encouraged to "seek authority figures to solve their problems and shield them from discomfort, a condition sociologists call 'moral dependency' where they can no longer think for themselves and fear offending someone to the point where they have to call in 'authority' figures to do the 'dirty work' for them?"[83]

Sometimes it is beneficial to have challenges and upsets early on in life to learn that life isn't fair, that there will be haters, bullies, and trolls who will try to knock you down, but it is your job to learn how to get back up and succeed, not to wait for someone to pick you up or do the work for you. Exposure to struggles early in life may help one build resiliency. This resiliency concept may be explained in terms of recommended inoculations. We are given shots at various intervals throughout our lifespan, in order for our bodies to build up a tolerance, defense, or immunity to the virus or bacteria in the shot. Our immune system learns to recognize the germ and creates a way to respond to it. In life, when we are exposed to various events, our brain is, ideally, building up a list of ways to respond to those situations; it is like a medicine chest or tool box of coping skills.

The cons of not "immunizing" ourselves either mentally or physically is that when an incident occurs, we may be ill-prepared for it. With an illness, it may have a more significant impact on our well-being. An example might be, for adults who acquire chicken pox, it can be fatal, but as children, they may have survived it without complication. Just as the body learns how to respond to a biological attack, children and teens should be given the opportunity to learn how to respond to life's psychological and social challenges or attacks. Isn't it best for them to "fail" or make a mistake while they are children and still at home instead of as an adult away at college?

Another aspect is to think of various events creating a "thicker" skin. It isn't saying that they should become jaded, but they shouldn't be naïve or overly sensitive, either. Challenging events, whether at home or at school, may lead to the development of emotional maturity. Counseling patients who have been exposed to divorce, substance use by a parent, death of a parent, abuse, or other difficult situations have had, through necessity, matured. Of course, we are not advocating for actively exposing a child to traumatic or upsetting events, but if they occur, we prefer dealing with them head on and not avoiding the reality of them. Political correctness, though, proposes the opposite. It heightens the sensitivity threshold, and prevents children from learning how to face life's challenges. When faced with challenges, we want to develop individuals who can "think on their feet" and not become immobilized with self-doubt, anxiety, or apathy, as an overly politically correct culture may have them develop.

How are schools who allow for retakes and late assignments teaching good study skills and time management? What lesson is it potentially teaching to students? Why has the bar been lowered for students to do the bare minimum and pass when success in the world is typically dictated by the amount of effort you put into a project? How is a student's self-confidence affected when he or she knows that they passed only because the expectation bar was lowered, and essentially, the school stating to students that we don't think that they are capable or smart enough to work at a higher, more responsible level? When that student goes into a more competitive environment where the bar is set at a different level, how will he or she respond? Colleges set admission deadlines. Bosses set project deadlines. Neither group is likely to waiver from the timelines and the standards they set for applicants. At some point, students must learn time management and the consequences of having poor management. If not in school, then when?

Isn't it a disservice or even cruel for students to leave school and not have the basic skills of time management, organization, and taking responsibility for their actions because their parents or school have enabled them? Sadly, it seems that some students may try to abuse programs that were intended for those who truly need the assistance by claiming some type of inequality and the need for those same accommodations. Is it possible that some politically correct laws that were meant to help those who really needed help to have become abused by allowing excuses for those who do not wish to take responsibility for their own actions?

Substance abuse, eating disorders, self-injury, and suicide

When political correctness policies and mindset go from a good concept that was meant to help those in need and becomes manipulated by man to serve his own gains, then the trickledown effect of such selfishness may be costing people their lives and limbs. Is it stating with absolute certainty that political correctness causes substance use, eating disorders, self-injury, suicides, or even murder? No! Correlation is *not* necessarily causation. However, there are enough correlations for you to take note of the possible ramifications of the mindset and policies.

There has been an increase in the number of teen suicides during the last 10 years. What is so different about this world and its pressures that were not present 20 or 30 years ago? Maybe it isn't so much that the pressures have changed, as our ability to deal with them.

Professional experience with thousands of patients and case consults has shown that control issues are a common theme for those who participate in eating disorders, substance abuse, self-injury, and unhealthy perfectionism. In *A Practitioner's Training in the Treatment of Self-injury: tips, techniques, activities, and debates,*[84] a discussion of how control was a common theme for both eating disorders and self-injury (NSSI) was addressed. In both instances, patients feel like everything around them is out of their control, that everyone else gets to "call the shots," and the only thing that they do control is what they can personally do to their own bodies. What if someone felt that he or she could not express his or her opinion for fear of potentially offending someone? Losing a job? Being harassed for not going along with the crowd? Could not going along with a P.C. policy lead to bullying? In those instances, would it be possible for someone to feel out of control and maybe stressed or anxious?

How does one start these behaviors? Imagine a soda bottle. Someone vigorously shakes it up and the pressure is clearly visible. Some may step away from it for fear that it might lose its top at any moment and spew the contents everywhere. Sometimes people are like soda bottles, but with the exception that often times we may not see all of the pressure building up inside. Think about how many times people interviewed on the news stating in disbelief that the perpetrator of a mass shooting, suicide, or some other type of violence was "quiet," "kept to themselves," "seemed a little odd," "thought they were a good kid," "never would have guessed what they were up to," etc.

Ideally, we should be gradually releasing that built up pressure each and every day. However, have there ever been times when it felt like that pressure couldn't escape? What if it were at a school or a job where each day there was a sense of apprehension as to who may get offended today or what new office policy will go into place, as a way to avoid another possible frivolous law suit? What if the pressure kept building for someone? Students who care about grades and their future academic life also stress over their social lives. Throw in any potential familial issue and lack of healthy coping skills, and then maybe you can start to see how people may not choose the healthiest course of action.

Substance use has long been a staple of the "trying to cope with life" mindset. Go back and watch television shows from the 1950s—how many of the male characters came home and had a cocktail to take the edge off of the day? In today's world, how many commercials, movies, songs, and TV shows reinforced the idea of using a substance to "deal" with life? And what did parents role model to their kids who then may have repeated the same behaviors? It has been documented that substance abuse by a caregiver affects the risk of the child repeating the same patterns. For example, if a parent smoked, the child has an increased risk of smoking because it has been normalized.

You may not have considered this, but isn't substance use another form of self-injury—just internal scaring instead of outward, visible scars? Eating disorders are another form of self-harm, too. With all three behaviors, there are individuals who are experiencing some emotional trigger and are looking for a way to escape it or the unpleasant feelings that accompany an event. A quick way to think of it is as follows:

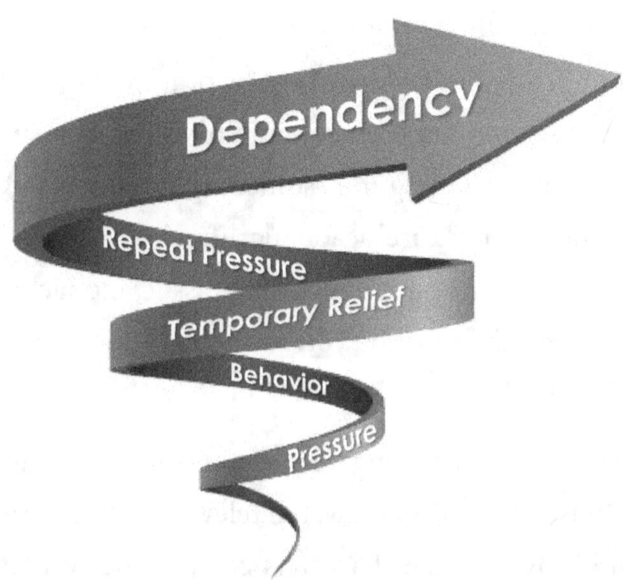

Figure 21: Vicious cycle

The behaviors may lose their potency; the user of them may develop a tolerance and will need to either seek out a more intense level of the behavior or find a new one. This can occur with the "flip flop" between eating *disorders* and *self-injury*, when one is "under control" then the other increases.

At some point, the person may get discouraged that they are either trapped by the need for those behaviors and/or feel they have lost their value. When the "coping" behavior no longer works, things begin to seem hopeless. When someone has lost hope, feels that the behavior is now controlling them, and a desire to try any new skills is gone, then suicidal thoughts tend to follow.

Isn't human nature such that we seek to alleviate any undue pressure or to flee an uncomfortable situation? What happens if the escapes that you have relied upon no longer work? What if you don't see your circumstances ever changing? Does death become, in the depressed person's mindset, the "easier option" or "the less painful" option? We are not stating that the mindset or policies of political correctness directly cause suicide, but we encouraging you to understand that there may be an unintended consequence of those thoughts and mindsets that contribute to some individuals deciding to take their own lives. Obviously, many variables play a role in why someone would harm himself or herself, and in this book, we are asking you to consider this particular piece of the puzzle.

Impact on society

A recent study in *Pediatrics*,[85] the journal of the American Academy of Pediatrics, found a nearly 50% increase in adolescent depression over the past 11 years.[86] With an approximate life time risk for Non-Suicidal Self-Injury (NSSI) ranging from 10% to 35%, suicide being the third leading cause of death for 10 to 14-year olds,[87] second leading cause of death for ages 15-24,[88] and that for every one suicide completion there are 25 attempts (source: *American Foundation for Suicide Prevention*), it is not *if* the reader will be touched by someone who has harmed or attempted, it is *when*.

What if we could help reduce a few factors that may contribute to these behaviors? Wouldn't that be worth looking into? Intervention is important. A Cornell University study showed that there is a 12-month window to intervene with someone who self-harms before they attempt suicide.[89] Over the past 10 years, there has been an increase in suicide attempts. Although all age groups showed an increase, the rate among women, particularly adolescent girls, took a notable jump. In 2012, suicide was the second leading cause of death in adolescents ages 12 to 19 years."[90]

Based upon almost 20 years of professional experience working with this population, we estimate that a minimum of 60% of those with a history of self-injury also have a history of suicidal thoughts or attempts. According to *Healthyplace.com*, those who self-harm were "nine times more likely to report suicide attempts" and "seven times more likely to report a suicidal gesture."[91]

By the rapid development and proliferation of substance abuse treatment centers, it is probably fair to state that the abuse of substances has also increased. A report by the *Substance Abuse and Mental Health Services Administration* (SAMHSA) stated, "The number of opioid treatment programs in the United States increased by 39 percent from 2003 to 2016."[92]

It isn't just opioids; it is substance use as a whole that is of concern, based on this information. "In 2016, approximately 20.1 million people aged 12 or older had a *Substance Use Disorder* (SUD) in the past year, including 15.1 million people who had an alcohol use disorder and 7.4 million people who had an illicit drug use disorder."[93]

Financial and safety implications

The more individuals attempt suicide or use substances as a way to try to cope, the more of a financial burden there is on our taxed health care system. Frequently, behavioral health hospitals reach their maximum capacity and do not have any beds for new patients. Many individuals do not get proper care due to cost of services, lack of available quality resources for them to use, and stigma. These individuals then go to work or school, where they may be less productive, irritable, cause conflicts or disruptions, and more likely to make mistakes. Some workers may go on disability, which costs the business money and stresses the other employees who must pick up the workload from the missing individual. The pressure builds at work or school and without proper resources, they risk having an emotional break down, which can take the form of getting into a fight, substance use or a suicide attempt at the location, or even bring a weapon with a plan to use it if anyone bothers them.

Add to the mix that someone in this state of mind feels mistreated, feels discriminated against, or that someone else was given the job that they felt they had worked for, and you have a potential powder keg waiting to explode. When someone is under the influence of a substance or severely depressed, how they view people may change; instead of humans, maybe they are seen as points or tasks in a game to be achieved. The dehumanization side effect of political correctness only increases that mindset. Finally, there is evidence that repeated exposure to violence through the media changes a person's perception of it; they become desensitized to it or jaded.

> Aggression is a trait that develops together with the nervous system over time starting from childhood. Patterns of [behavior] become solidified and the nervous system prepares to continue the [behavior] patterns into adulthood when they become increasingly coached in personality.
>
> This could be at the root of the differences in people who are aggressive and non-aggressive - and how media motivates them to do certain things.[94]

A study by the Indiana University School of Medicine examined young men and violent media exposure. There were visible alterations in MRI brain scans after only one week of playing a violent video game.[95]

Forced by political correctness and office policies designed to make everyone equal may not have created a sense of equality, but an "us versus them" mindset. The disgruntled, depressed, angry worker who resents the policies or the peers he perceives as getting the "perks" may start to dehumanize his perceived "competition." Once you dehumanize someone, it becomes easier to not care about his or her wellbeing. If the person feels desperate and thinks that his or her survival is at stake, whether real or imagined, then he or she become dangerous. It is this fear aspect that governments have sometimes used to turn people against one another. Fear is a very powerful motivator. If you see another person as a threat, then "taking out" an enemy is not as reprehensible.

Adulting

A student has graduated college and now must enter into the "real world" and become a true adult. Armed with a degree and an air of confidence, the new group of students sends out their resumes expecting to find jobs that start at $50,000 a year, plus benefits, because, after all, they are graduates and they "deserve" to be compensated for their time in school. But wait… not every college graduate will get hired, and of those who do, the majority will not start off with a $50,000 a year job, but possibly $30,000 or less. The bubble bursts. Some students actually believe, or at least act as if they are entitled to have a job that meets all of their criteria, even though they do not have the level of training or experience commensurate with the salary they think they should have to fit the lifestyle they think that they should have. Some of them, being shielded from the realities of the world, don't even know how much they need to live comfortably.

And then there is yet another shocking reality check for those who have been sheltered by schools that allow for re-tests and extended deadlines—there are deadlines in the workplace; the boss doesn't care that you had a bad day, that you stayed up late binge watching a show, that your political candidate didn't win the election, or that you "just didn't feel like doing it" as acceptable reasons for a missed deadline. The stunned college graduate may complain about how unreasonable their boss is in setting deadlines that they did not get to pick or have a say in, or that they have to work on a project that they do not feel passionate about or necessarily agree with.

As with every generation, there are always going to be some workers who feel that they should automatically receive certain positions, promotions, or raises regardless of the amount of work they have exerted or the skills they have displayed. When these entitled employees don't get what they want, they cry foul and make various retaliatory threats. In today's workplace, threats mean money. Whether the cost to the business is due to decreased product sales because of negative reviews, a complaint filed by a State or Federal agency, or a hostile work environment lawsuit, companies must now make tough decisions as to which is the lesser of two evils— pay off the employee, give them whatever they want (short term gain with a long term consequence), or risk losing thousands upon thousands of dollars in litigation fees. Employees, who have learned how to manipulate the system, usually starting during their school years, will continue to take advantage of, and abuse the laws that were designed to protect those employees who are truly in need of them until some cultural shift fights back against such "entitled" attitude.

Yet another dose of reality for some students is that not everyone is kind and understanding, that when you are stressed out or offended, there are no "safe places" to run and hide at. In search of some way to cope with the flood of emotions from these circumstances, they may turn to substance abuse as their method for decreasing their discomfort. While it could be the more "traditional" forms of substances, such as alcohol and cigarette smoking, it may escalate to the use of Benzodiazepines such as Xanax, Klonopin, Ativan, or "old school" Valium. Unless they work through the thoughts, reactions, and issues behind those emotions, they may risk continuing to rely upon substances as their way of coping with life.

Patients, particularly those in their early to mid-20s, started to use the term "adulting," as in it is difficult to be an adult with all of the expectations and demands that adulthood entails, and they no longer want to be adults; they want to regress back to a time when they had little to no responsibility. However, they still want the adult privileges, such as drinking, smoking, going out with friends, staying up as late as they want, having their own cars, their freedom, etc.; they are just unwilling to pay for it. In essence, these "twenty-somethings" still want to be teenagers. Many who fail at "adulting" end up on their parents' couches not paying rent for the next six months, or even many, many years.

What are the problems associated with "adulting?" There is a lack of coping mechanisms at a domestic and professional level, they get overwhelmed, some emotional immaturity is present, they emotionally shut down when confronted about their plans, and they lack motivation or choices. The confrontations are responded to with a mix of anxiety and/or depression with some verbal aggression or defensiveness sprinkled in for good measure. They may respond with comments such as, "who are *you* to judge me," "I feel triggered," "you can't tell me what to do, stop trying to make me conform to your ideas," or some variation of these remarks. It is important to note that they may truly feel hopeless, even helpless, and when they get to that point, suicide may look like an option, as a permanent escape from short-term problems.

Part 2: 1969
The Causes of Political Correctness

CHAPTER 10

Compliance with Authority

Not too many major changes in our nation or culture could be tracked to a single event or day in history. World War I is attributed to the assassination of Archduke Franz Ferdinand of Austria-Hungary in Sarajevo on June 28, 2914. While this might have been the trigger event, other factors such as the mutual defense alliances, imperialism, militarism, and nationalism caused a pent-up pressure that the trigger assassination released. The same can be said for the U.S. involvement in World War II. The Japanese attack on Pearl Harbor on December 7, 1941 was the trigger event, forcing President Roosevelt to declare war on the Axis alliance, although additional factors, even as far as the Great Depression, played a role.

In this book, we will show that there was such a trigger event that caused the rise of political correctness in our culture to the levels it exists today. One event, one evening, almost 50 years ago.

***

As our definition of *Political Correctness* suggests, we relinquish our right and responsibility to determine what is acceptable or appropriate behavior (*by* us and *towards* us) to people with authority over us. In other words—we are politically correct because we are told by others we should be. To begin this discussion, we start by identifying those people of authority. The Merriam-Webster dictionary defines authority as "Power to influence or command thought, opinion, or behavior."[96]

Who has such authority over us? To answer that, we turn to the *Maslow's Hierarchy of Needs* theory (1943, 1954).[97] It suggests five layers of needs we have, starting with the most fundamental: physiological needs (air, shelter, food, water, warmth, and rest). Once you achieved those, you turn to achieve the second level: safety needs (security, safety). The third level includes belonging and love needs. The fourth level includes self-esteem needs. Finally, once all the needs below it were achieved, you turn to the fifth level: self-actualization needs. The first two levels (physiological and safety) are referred to as *basic needs*. The next two levels (belonging and love, self-esteem) are called *psychological* needs, and the last one (self-actualization) is call the *self-fulfillment* needs.

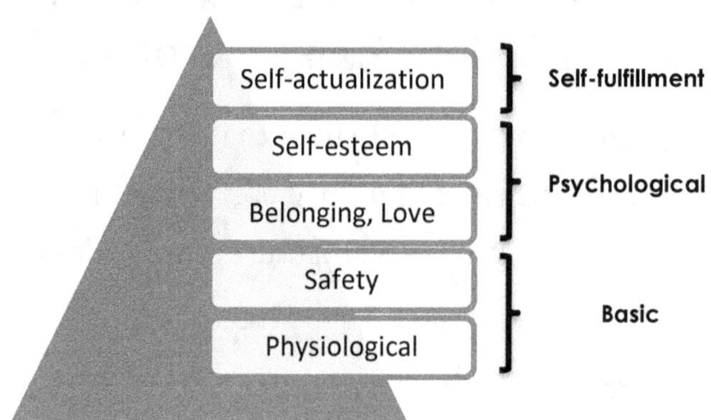

Figure 22: Maslow's hierarchy of needs

With the understanding of those levels, it is now clear to recognize who has authority over us—those who can control our ability to fulfill our needs. Those include our—

- Employers
- Schools
- Government
- Media
- Celebrities
- Family and friends

If you don't think that people of authority (and thus control over your life) can have such an impact on what you do (or don't do), just follow the recent wave of sexual harassment cases, where someone in authority (such as a film producer) forced people whose career, financial well-being, or anything else were controlled by that person to do something they really didn't want to.

Social psychology

In any introduction to psychology class or social psychology class, the famous, or maybe infamous, Milgram Experiment is taught. The researcher, Stanley Milgram at Yale University, "examined justifications for acts of genocide offered by those accused at the World War II, Nuremberg War Criminal trials. Their defense often was based on "obedience" - that they were just following orders from their superiors."[98]

The essence of Milgram's experiment was to see what people were willing to do to other human beings under the guise of obedience to perceived authority. It also taught us that assumptions about people and their level of influence is dangerous, and that sometimes we may just be surprised when we choose to confront those who we believe we should fear.

Imagine a clinical-type lab environment where you have the actor in a white lab coat, another actor (student) pretending to receive shocks from a machine, and the subject (teacher) who had no idea that he was participating in a social psychology experiment, and that the other two are researchers-actors, and not what he believes them to be. The subject was asked to give a mild electric shock to the student each time he did not answer a question correctly; the student-actor faked a physical response to make the subject think that the shocks were real. Each time the student missed a question, the level of shock increased, with the highest being marked as "severe shock" at 450 volts. The actor in the lab coat only gives verbal prods to encourage the subject (teacher) to continue with the shocks, but there are no threats, no coercion to comply, and no perceived consequences if non-compliant.

The results were disturbing. Approximately two thirds of the teachers administered the highest level of shock, 450 volts. All of them administered, what they thought, was a 300 volt shock, marked "danger." The conclusion was that "people tend to obey orders from other people if they recognize their authority as *morally right* and/or *legally based.* This response to legitimate authority is learned in a variety of situations, for example in the family, school, and workplace."[99] However, there are some variables that can alter the influence of authority in compliance, such as the location of the authority figure (whether they were in the room or was the orderly called in), others defying the authority figure, the location of the event (a lab versus a dirty office), and "when there is less personal responsibility obedience increases." The latter is similar in nature

140

to the *Diffusion of Responsibility* concept that is exemplified in the *Kitty Genovese* case, which will be described later in this chapter.

***

Another experiment testing compliance to authority figures was conducted in a hospital by C.K. Hofling and is simply referred to as the *Hofling Hospital Experiment.*

"Hofling demonstrated that people are very unwilling to question supposed "authority," even when they might have good reason to." He found that 21 out of 22 nurses broke three of the hospitals rules because a reported doctor called them and asked them to do so. The results were disconcerting because it helped demonstrate just how willing people are to obey perceived authority without asking questions, even if they know it is breaking the rules.[100] Can we think of some examples in today's world where people follow a perceived person in power and do their bidding without asking questions? There are examples of people who think they are prophets, foreign political leaders, and social media "stars" who throw out dangerous challenges. Even in academia.

In political correctness gone amuck, society is given guidelines, rules, and policies as to how to act, what to see, and how to feel. To deviate from those things puts the person at risk of being an outcast. If the messages are being disseminated from a business organization, government officials, or celebrities, then those can be seen as people in positions of perceived authority. Is it not possible, just like in Milgram's experiment, that if we are told we should be offended by something, then we are more likely to become offended?

Many will not question the statements or from whom they come from, but rather blindly accept those statements. Those who try to "buck the system" may be met with "prods" like in either the experiment or the actual pressure or coercion to comply. When those who used to believe one thing, then change to another position that happens to be "in vogue" or popular, they will say that they have a new "enlightened" perspective, which may be true or they may have had some social psychology get to them.

Diffusion of responsibility

As discovered in Milgram's experiment, when we believe that we are the only one who feels a certain way, hold off acting on our feeling until we see others feeling the same way. Furthermore, if we see several other people observing the same situation that we are, we assume that someone else will act upon that situation and that it isn't our responsibility to intervene, which is referred to as *diffusion of responsibility*. For Milgram, it was blaming the actor in the lab coat for their actions. In the case of diffusion of responsibility, it is blaming others for not acting because they could have done something just as easily as we could. The diffusion is an assumption—it assumes that someone else will do the job, so you can rationalize remaining passive.

In 1964, a young woman named Kitty Genovese was brutally murdered while 38 people were watching from the safety of their homes. The murderer brutally attacked her and left her at the scene of the attack for quite some time before coming back to continue and torture Kitty until she died. Yet, not a single person called the police. How could this be? Simply put, everyone assumed that somebody else had called the authorities. However, the next logical question would be: why, after ten minutes of witnessing the events and no police showed up, didn't someone call the police then? Or go down to check on her ten minutes after the assailant had left the scene?

When we stop taking personal responsibility for our actions and the potential impact that we have on others, then we run the serious risk of chaos ensuing, which may include dehumanization, substance related crimes, theft, and many more serious consequences. For some aspects of P.C., there seems to be a slant of "it's OK, it's not your fault, we will fix things for you, you are just a victim of…" As billionaire Bill Gates, has reportedly said, "If you are *born* poor, that's not your fault, but if you *die* poor, it's your fault." In America, there are countless stories of success of people born into poverty that developed into powerhouses of influence. People who have truly defied the odds of what was expected of them and refused to be passive, not give into their environments, and actively fought against their friends', families', and society's low expectations of them. Some would say that they did not see equality as the final resting place, but rather as a stop on the way to success. It isn't that they saw themselves as superior human beings, but they recognized that they have untold potential that can either be used or go to waste; they have decided to not abdicate that responsibility for another person or circumstance to decide their fate.

However, on the opposite end of taking ownership of one's actions and fate, are those who give away, either passively or actively, their skills, potential, livelihood, and hope. Some have been told that they are victims and need to rely upon others for survival. While this may be true in the case of natural disasters, unexpected medical expenses, crimes, or extreme circumstances, it is not true in everyday life. A concern with political correctness is that there are some who may believe that they are "special" and need ongoing extra assistance, that they can't do things on their own without *continuous* help; they need rules, exceptions, rallies, and policies to help them get out of their unfortunate, compromised situation. Before you start to recite a list of groups that need these exceptions, keep reading and defer your judgment.

While many advances have taken place over the centuries in promoting equality, there is still a need to address discrimination, inequality, and promote education about those with physical or mental challenges. Education is one step to help even out the playing field. However, at the same time, could it come across as condescending and demoralizing that the group "needs special treatment," which is not the intent of the policies, but may be an unintended consequence? The result could be that some may have decreased motivation to try new things if they feel that they *need* to have someone pave the way for them. Some may not like feeling "different" and needing special accommodations. As with all things, there is always a balance to be had between helping those individuals who need and seek help and providing resources for them, but without compromising their confidence, ingenuity, motivation, curiosity, empowerment, or drawing undue attention to them where they feel singled out versus included.

Another aspect of diffusion of responsibility and the role of obedience to authority figures, is the "passing the liability game" in companies. The employee manual is part guideline for how to act and part, "if something goes wrong, blame can be passed on to the company or employee." An employee may falsely assume that everything in the manual is fine because other people have read it, "if it is good enough for *them* to sign, then it's alright to comply with it, too…" and it goes unread. The employee does not question the authority of those who put the manual together. He diffuses his responsibility by assuming others did their due diligence in reviewing it and if there were any potential problems, that they would have been corrected by the time the new employee received the manual. As time passes, the new employee is unlikely to have read the manual. When an issue arises at work, the employee may be quick to blame management, HR, and a slew of others for the problem, but may fail to take personal responsibility for his or her actions. The same can be said for the "Terms and Conditions" contract that you are asked to accept when accessing certain online content, downloading software, and the like. At the end of this book we included our own "Terms and Conditions" section, as well. You should read it. Really. It is often stated that ignorance of the law is no excuse for breaking it, so it can be assumed that it wouldn't apply to the work place, either. In the next chapter, we will review the other side of this problem, too.

The Legal Bar and the Ethical Bar

In his book *Mere Christianity,*[101] British author Clive Staples (C.S.) Lewis (1898-1963) wrote: "You cannot make men good by law: and without good men you cannot have a good society."

To understand how we are controlled by increasing regulations and policies, consider the following. Your possible actions in any situation range from the worst you can do (bottom) to the best you can do (top). There is a spectrum of actions in between the two. Another dimension for those actions is the "others-to-self" benefit ratio. The higher that ratio is (the more your actions benefit *others* than they benefit *you*), the higher your actions rate on that spectrum. The lower the ratio (the more your actions benefit *you* than they benefit *others*), the lower your actions rate on the spectrum.

Figure 23: The legal bar and the ethical bar

Now imagine that there is a legal bar, and somewhere *above* it—an ethical bar. To clarify, when we refer to the legal bar, we include not only the constitution and federal and state laws, but also local regulations, as well as policies, such as those created by your employer or school. Actions you might take *below* the *legal* bar are, well, illegal. Some of those illegal activities may carry negative consequences for you, whether a fine, jail time, or even capital punishment, depending on how low were your actions on that spectrum. Actions you take *above* the *ethical* bar are, for the lack of a better word, good. Some of those are simply ethical; while others show significant sacrifice, willingness to serve no matter how harsh the circumstances are (such as serving on a school board…) The actions on the absolute top of that continuum may reward you with military awards, high civilian recognition, or even sainthood.

The legal bar, as set by laws, policies, and regulations is strict and controlled by others (your government, employer, or school). Therefore, following them (staying above the legal bar) is somewhat involuntary; you still have a choice for non-compliance, but you will have to accept the consequences. You take those actions not because they are the right thing to do—you take them because you are told to, and because there are negative personal consequences to you if you don't. The motivation to comply with those regulations is extrinsic. It has nothing to do with how good (or bad) those actions are. However, the higher your actions rank on that spectrum, the more voluntary they become. Your government, employer, or school may force you to act above the legal bar, but not higher than that. Acting above it is your choice. The motivation to do better and better things, even when nobody forces you to and there are no consequences, is intrinsic. You are motivated by the positive outcome (typically to others) of your actions.

So what do you call the area between the legal bar and the ethical bar? Actions that are below the ethical bar, while above the legal bar? Well, there are many names for those areas. Those are the type of things you know you *shouldn't* do, but you do them anyway, because they are not illegal. Those are "loopholes." Behaviors that the governing bodies haven't yet identified as bad, and haven't created laws, policies, or regulations to prevent you from doing them.

How can we prevent you (or anyone else, for that matter), from performing those things that are below the ethical bar, albeit above the legal bar? The best way would be to somehow *motivate* people to perform above the ethical bar. However, governing bodies don't like leaving anything to your discretion. What do they do? They raise the legal bar. Here is an example. Corporate financial scandals escalated at the turn of the century. Those included *Enron*, *Tyco International*, *Adelphia*, *Peregrine Systems*, and *WorldCom*, to name a few. Some of the actions top executives in those companies took were illegal even then, for which a few were sentenced to prison. But to prevent actions which were above the legal bar at the time (albeit deep below the ethical bar) from occurring again, Congress enacted laws such as *The Public Company Accounting Reform and Investor Protection Act*, known as *Sarbanes-Oxley*, in 2002. The government took the easy route. Since corporate executives are not to be trusted with staying above the ethical bar, we would raise the legal bar, and put consequences for going below it.

For clarification purposes, many organizations have ethical codes or standards that their members are bound by. Those are sometimes called professional conduct codes. Don't get confused by the use of the word "ethical" in the name of those codes. Those are regulations, or policies, and do not mark the ethical bar. When there are possible extrinsic negative consequences for violating them (such as termination of membership, disbarment, etc.), they stop acting as a voluntary ethical bar and act exactly the same as rules, regulations, and policies.

The consequences of *Sarbanes-Oxley* were severe for Corporate America. Public companies and their executives face dramatically increasing workloads just to stay in compliance with those regulations. Companies prefer not to become public, as a way to avoid that increased paperwork, workload, and cost. The number of Initial Public Offerings (IPO) declined from 300 a year before 2000 to 100 a year since then. Public companies have chosen to go back to being private. There were 7,322 public companies traded in the U.S. Stock Exchanges in 1996. There were only 3,671 public companies in 2017.[102]

But increased regulation has even more significant social-cultural consequences. The more regulations we have, the higher the legal bar is, the more we become motivated extrinsically by the personal consequences to ourselves, rather than the consequences to others. We become less intrinsically motivated. We become less driven by the overall good for society. We are less driven by the ethical bar and more by the legal bar. As a result, more of our actions fall below the ethical bar (albeit above the legal bar). To avoid the cognitive dissonance associated with acting below "what's right" (the ethical bar), we drag the ethical bar lower. We define the new ethical bar such that it will deem our actions as good.

As a result, we do things because we are told to, not because they make sense. For example, public school districts have policy manuals with more than 1,000 pages. Company employee manuals are hundreds of pages long. It becomes unreasonable for employees to know all the policies they are subject to (the legal bar), even though violating some of those may cause their termination.

So we continue to raise the legal bar, removing any need to maintain an ethical bar and stay above it. But do you think that there could ever be a time when the legal bar would actually rise above the ethical bar? While it doesn't sound possible—it is. Let's think about what it means to act *above* the ethical bar. Those actions may be called *good, selfless,* and many other things, but in general we can refer to them as *legitimate.* So, what would happen when the legal bar rises above the ethical bar? And, more importantly—what kind of actions would be above the ethical bar, yet below the new legal bar?

You don't have to think too hard. Did you ever drive your car above the speed limit? You don't need to answer that… When did driving over the speed limit become legitimate? The law is very clear about it. You have done the opposite of what political correctness does. You took matters into your own hands. You replaced the strict definition of the law with your own judgment. And that is a slippery slope, which starts when the legal bar is raised above the ethical bar, instead of trying to keep the ethical bar high enough, and assuring that we act above it.

Loopholes

Case in point, on October 1, 2017, 64-year-old Stephen Paddock opened fire from his room on the 32nd floor of the Mandalay Bay hotel in Las Vegas, aiming at the participants of the *Route 91 Harvest Music Festival.* In the ten minutes between 10:05 and 10:15 PM he fired 1,100 rounds from his rifles, killing 58 people and injuring 851 more attendees. Witnesses reported hearing full-automatic gun fire. Of the 24 guns that were found in his hotel room, 14 were equipped with a *bump stock.*[103] The incident drew attention to that device, which allowed converting a semi-automatic rifle into a fully-automatic one, in a legal way. There is no doubt that Paddock's ability to shoot that many rounds in such a short time, before the police stormed his room, played a major role in making this the deadliest mass-shooting in American history until the time of writing this book.

Federal law makes it illegal for any private civilian to own any fully-automatic weapons manufactured after May 19, 1986.[104] That law and the prohibition on owning fully-automatic weapons existed long before Paddock checked into his hotel room. So why could he still fire in fully-automatic mode using the bump stocks, and in a legal way?

The answer to this question comes down to the legal definition of a fully-automatic firearm, or a *machine gun.* The definition is found in 26 U.S.C. § 5845(b) as "Any weapon which shoots, is designed to shoot, or can be readily restored to shoot, automatically more than one shot without manual reloading, by a single function of the trigger."[105] The "loop hole" here is the last half sentence: "by a single function of the trigger." The way bump stocks work is by allowing the entire weapon to move back and forth against the shooter's finger, thus causing multiple trigger actions in a very short time, without the shooter ever moving the trigger finger.[106] An audio analysis of a Las Vegas video showed that in the span of ten seconds, Paddock fired 90 shots, or nine shots per second. A full-automatic Colt AR-15A2, built as a military machine gun, shoots 14 rounds per second. Not a significant difference. Given this high rate of fire, Paddock shot 1,100 bullets.[107] At the rate of nine rounds per second, and with very large capacity magazines, it is not inconceivable that he could have fired more than 5,000 rounds in those ten minutes it took the police to stop him.

No doubt, we appreciate American ingenuity. However, did the inventors of the bump stock not know that their device can be used to turn a legal semi-automatic rifle into a fully-automatic rifle? The answer to that is clearly *yes*, as can be seen from the first words in the patent covering the bump stock: "A method for *rapidly* [our emphasis] firing a semi-automatic firing unit."[108] Did they not realize that the law prohibited the use of machine guns? Although we cannot speak to what exactly they thought, it is clear to us that they found the loophole in the legal definition of the prohibited machine gun, and used it. And then Stephen Paddock used it.

As we are writing these lines, President Trump declared his intention to ban bump stocks. However, it's just like playing "Whacka-mole." Why? Because if we ban the use of bump stocks, another brilliant American inventor will find another loophole that will allow turning a legal weapon into a full-automatic one. This all happens because we continue to raise the legal bar, instead of promoting the use of common sense and high ethical behavior.

CYA

How often have you had to click the "I accept" or "I agree" button before purchasing something online, downloading a software application, or even accessing your online bank account? Quite often, right? Now, be honest—how often do you actually read the agreement that you have just accepted? The answer is most likely "not very often," if at all. When you sign up to the BlueCross BlueShield online service, you have to click the button at the bottom indicating that you have read and agreed to the website's Terms of Use. It is a 3,483-word document that spans over seven pages. It is filled with legal language that the average consumer would not understand. Yet you are asked to sign that you have read it, understood it, and agree to it.

When you are employed by a company, you are required to read and agree to the employee policy manual, code of conduct, or any other similar document. As an employee in a Texas independent school district, you are expected to know the policies of your district. There are more than 1,000 pages to that policy manual. You are required to sign a document that states that you agree to be bound by those policies. But have you really read those documents before you signed them? You don't need to answer…

Take a look at a typical TV commercial. The last few seconds have text in tiny print. The average adult's reading speed is 200 to 300 words per minute. There is absolutely no way for you to read that text at the end of the commercial. Often, claims are made in the commercial (or ad) that are countered or reduced in that section of small print. An example is a newspaper ad made by Dell in 2011, touting their XPS-15 laptop as "the thinnest 15" PC on the planet." The small print, though, specifically stated that no comparison was made to Apple or other manufacturers not listed. Take a look at the CashCall.com loan TV advertisement. The last 5 seconds of the commercial, in small print, hold 106 words, which would take an average adult at least 20 seconds to read (if the TV resolution would even allow you to read such small print). Those words include the fact that the interest rate on such a typical loan would be 99.25% annually![109] The same applies to the disclaimers at the end of a radio commercial, when the size of the words is replaced with lower volume, but the speed in which they are read make the disclaimers incomprehensible.

When you visit your physician or a clinic, you are asked to sign a form in which you declare that you were given, understood, and agreed to the privacy practices of that clinic, per HIPAA requirements. Have you received the privacy policy document? Did you read it? Did you understand it?

Why do they do that?

There are two simple reasons. One is that we have a culture of litigation, as you will read in the next chapter. We are simply afraid we will get sued. A customer may sue us for the 99.25% interest rate, if we didn't mention it anywhere. However, when they do, our defense would be that we did disclose such information, ignoring the fact that it was in such a small print, low volume, and so fast that it was not reasonable to comprehend.

The second reason, though, is because due to the continual raising of the legal bar (to compensate for a continuous erosion of the ethical bar), we do things because the law requires us to, and not because we believe we should act as ethical standards would dictate. It is a very clear case of allowing our judgment to be replaced by somebody else's opinion or judgment. And that, again, is our definition of Political Correctness.

Plausible Deniability

In the movie *Independence Day*, the President is brought to a building that contained an alien spaceship. When he asked "why the hell wasn't I told about this place?" the answer was "two words, Mr. President: Plausible Deniability." One definition of this term is:

> [Plausible] deniability refers to circumstances where a denial of responsibility or knowledge of wrongdoing cannot be proved as true or untrue due to a lack of evidence proving the allegation. This term is often used in reference to situations where high ranking officials deny responsibility for or knowledge of wrongdoing by lower ranking officials. In those situations officials can "plausibly deny" an allegation even though it may be true. It also refers to any act that leaves little or no evidence of wrongdoing or abuse.[110]

Think about the meaning of this term. It allows someone to knowingly avoid acknowledging something, so that he could act as if that something didn't exist. As long as there is no way to prove that you knew something, and as long as your actions are not illegal if you didn't know it, then pretending you didn't know it clears you of any wrongdoing. That doesn't rank very high on the ethical scale, does it?

Zero Tolerance

Another symbol of our politically correct culture is the term *Zero Tolerance*. The term was first used in the June 1963 issue of *Popular Mechanics*. The article *And Was It a Silent Spring?* discussed what happened to wildlife, pets, bugs, and people as a result of pesticide use in Sheldon, Illinois. The article goes on to describe the FDA pesticide regulations, citing that the toxic ingredient Heptachlor was given a "zero tolerance" by the FDA, which meant that "not even the slightest trace of heptachlor [was] permitted on food."

The *Free Dictionary* offers the following definition for the term Zero Tolerance: "The policy of applying laws or penalties to even minor infringements of a code in order to reinforce its overall importance and enhance deterrence."[111]

The term was much more broadly used in the 1980s' war on drugs during the Reagan administration, and later legislated by Congress towards weapons on school grounds. From there, the term was used in more and more areas. In general, Zero Tolerance means that a certain activity will not be tolerated at any level, and that there is no excuse or defense that could be used against claims of that nature.

In 2012, the *American Bar Association* published an article[112] reviewing the use of Zero Tolerance policies in school and covered several cases on the issue. No longer was Zero Tolerance used against drug use or weapon carrying, but it was now extended to bullying and other expressions. *The Tinker v. Des Moines Independent Community School District* 1969 case limited the rights of schools in punishing students for certain expressions. Zero Tolerance was weighed against the first amendment right to free speech.

Regardless, the proliferation of the use of Zero Tolerance suggests something else: that once again, we abdicate our judgement to that of someone else, specifically to Zero Tolerance policies. No longer do we care about context or reasons. Again, we raise the legal bar instead of fighting to maintain the ethical bar from eroding. And that, once again, is our definition of Political Correctness.

Accredited Investor

On April 5, 2012, President Obama signed the *Jumpstart Our Business Startups (JOBS) Act* into law.[113] The purpose of the law was to encourage funding of small businesses (startups) in the U.S. by easing many of the SEC regulations. While many such regulations have been relaxed, one regulation under Title III of the law raises eyebrows. At least ours… The company may only raise investments up to $1,070,000 through *crowdfunding* in a 12-month period. An investor making an income less than $107,000 a year cannot invest more than 5% of that. An investor making more than $107,000 *and* has a net worth of more than $107,000 can invest up to 10% of the lower of the two values, but not more than $107,000 in a 12-month period.[114]

The hypocrisy of that? Anyone can spend 100% of their income and net worth on any stock, or in a casino. No restrictions whatsoever. The only restriction on how much you can invest is when you invest in a small business, which has the potential of contributing to the U.S. GDP and create jobs. Another example of how we raise the legal bar instead of allowing people to use judgement and common sense.

Group dynamics

Have you ever noticed that when one person enters into an ongoing group conversation, the entire dynamic of the group can change? It could be the vibe, the topic, the words used, the tone, or energy level. The group influences the individual, which could be seen as a majority rule situation, but many times, it can be the individual who influences the group; the minority impacts the majority. Remember a time when everyone was in an upbeat mood and then one person came along with some bad news, drama, or negative outlook and the energy was sucked out of the group? What happens when one person starts to complain in a group? Is it easier for the rest of the group to follow suit into a "gripe fest" or to try to resist the negativity and work on reframing something in a positive light?

"The interactions that influence the attitudes and behavior of people when they are grouped with others through either choice or accidental circumstances" is referred to as *group dynamics*, a term coined by Kurt Lewin.[115] The more exposure you get to a certain thought, perspective, or behavior, the less likely you are to object if you see others participating in the same behavior or thought process. Group dynamics and groupthink can also be associated with confirmation bias, where you only expose yourself to people who share your same views, thus falsely assuming that everyone must share your views. An example from the media would be if someone watches only one news station. Every opinion or news story from the source was taken at face value. The person socialized only with others who watched that same channel. It would be easy for that person to think that anyone who did not listen to that news channel was wrong and would avoid socializing with them.

Groupthink—"go along to get along"

Groupthink, a term coined by social psychologist Irving Janis (1972), occurs when a group makes faulty decisions because group pressures lead to a deterioration of "mental efficiency, reality testing, and moral judgment." Groups affected by groupthink ignore alternatives and tend to take irrational actions that could dehumanize other groups.[116]

From the time that we are aware that there are groups in the world, we want to feel like we belong to at least one—our in-group. Everyone wants to be part of a group; no one wants to be the outsider. With group think, there is a danger in being a part of only one group. Stories in the news about cults remind us of the dangers of groupthink or even recent events of governments that do not allow any other point of view but that which is sanctioned by the powers that be. Through incestuous amplification they "persuade" their followers to believe whatever propaganda they send out.

One interesting aspect of political correctness is that it is a bit of a reverse groupthink. Instead of the majority group ruling the thoughts of a society, it is the minority opinion that takes precedence. Eventually, it is the minority opinion that gains enough traction through various social psychology situations that it becomes the new perceived majority.

Stockholm syndrome

Are P.C. policies like captors for some people who don't even realize the consequences that they will experience? Let's examine the famous Stockholm syndrome case. On August 23, 1973, two armed robbers entered a Stockholm bank. They held four hostages for five days, strapping them with dynamite until their rescue on August 28. The surprising part was the behavior of the hostages after their release:

> The hostages exhibited a shocking attitude considering they were threatened, abused, and feared for their lives for over five days. In their media interviews, it was clear that they supported their captors and actually feared law enforcement personnel who came to their rescue. The hostages had begun to feel the captors were actually protecting them.
>
> In the final analysis, emotionally bonding with an abuser is actually a strategy for survival for victims of abuse and intimidation.[117]

In an odd twist of fate, sometimes victims start to identify with their captor, even possibly blaming themselves for being the victim and understanding the plight of their captor. Can this occur for people who may not have seen themselves as victims, but have been convinced that they are victims and then they take on that mindset, which, in turn, changes their level of motivation, their focus, and even their interactions with people that they once called friends? One could possible say in this case that, "you don't know what you don't know." If you do not know that you are a victim, "special," or need extra assistance, but then you are told that you are and need to, in some way, start acting more like a victim and even possibly give up some things that you had going for you; you might initially scoff at such an idea.

However, what if with time, propaganda, social pressures, etc., you start to see the people who are costing you money and status as actually being your saviors who will make things better? Does some version of this happen in politics when politicians keep enabling their constituents to stay on food stamps, provide a situation where it is more beneficial to stay on welfare than to maintain employment, and do not require drug tests in order to receive the funds? Employers require a drug test to stay employed, so why doesn't the government require the same thing? Shouldn't the government try to encourage people to become employed and stay off drugs? Or is there some other reason that the politicians would like to keep people in victim/dependent mode? Policies that are supposed to "help" people may actually be hurting them. When people keep voting for them, even though they are actually being hurt by them through increased poverty, crime, and few business opportunities, is that not an instantiation of the Stockholm effect?

Throwing away the title of "Special Needs"

What if people create issues that are not there? It is likely unintentional, but in the desire to make everyone equal by drawing attention to those that are not, could it be that some groups don't want to see themselves as needing help or as "special?" Is there the possibility that society and its rules are inadvertently creating a sense of inferiority among those it is trying to help? Frank Stepehens, a Quincy Jones Advocate for the Global Down Syndrome Foundation, is a man with Down syndrome himself, who testified before Congress as to how the group he represented wanted to be defined.[118] They were able to function in day-to-day life, had jobs, went to school, participated in social activities, etc. In their testimony, they rejected the term "special needs," disabled, and other like terms. In essence, they refused to let a diagnosis or a challenge define them or what they were capable of doing in their daily lives.

A Culture of Litigation

What are we afraid of?

In the two previous chapters we explained how we are significantly influenced by other people and organizations that have a perceived authority over our lives, and how they exert that power. You now understand the mechanisms. But one question is left open: why do those organizations that have authority over our lives force us to behave in certain ways? Why do they force us to be Politically Correct? Why can't they leave our behavior and actions at our discretion?

The answer is painfully simple—because they are afraid of being sued. In a closed session of a prominent school district board meeting, the legal counsel to the board warned the board members against taking a certain action. The reason was—there are plenty of lawyers that would find this "as a good enough reason as any" to sue you.

Those organizations (employers, schools, etc.) have "deep pockets." In other words, they have enough money and assets to pay if they lost a major lawsuit. People hardly sue other people. Not for a lot of money, at least. The reason is simple: individuals typically don't have a lot to sue them for. What's the point in suing an individual for $54 million? He may only have $10,000 in the bank, after which he will declare bankruptcy and that will be the end of your lawsuit; as a note, his lawyers would probably get paid before you, the plaintiff.

No, you want to sue those with deep pockets. They can pay. They will likely settle (only 2% of civil lawsuits actually get resolved in court),[119] but they can really pay a lot. We should also emphasize that we are talking about civil litigation, i.e., over alleged damages by one entity to another, rather than criminal (state v. criminal) or constitutional litigation

Are we really such a litigious society?

In 2011, the *U.S. Chamber's Institute for Legal Reform* showed that the U.S. is leading the developed world in liability costs as percentage of the Gross Domestic Product (GDP). The U.S. spends 1.66% of its GDP on liability costs. The second country is Canada, with 1.19%. Only one more country, the UK, spends more than 1% of its GDP on liability. The Eurozone average is 0.63%, and Japan spends 0.3%. As a percentage of GDP, The U.S. spends, relatively, 40% more than Canada, 58% more than the UK, 163% more than the European average, and 453% more than Japan.[120] In Dollar value, the U.S. spends on civil litigation almost twice as much as Canada, the UK, the entire Eurozone, and Japan, combined; not something for the U.S. to brag about.

The report adds another variable: the legal environment. It is defined as "*a linear combination of whether or not the legal system is based on civil or common law, and the number of lawyers per capita in the country.*" The U.S. takes top place as having the worst legal environment. The *Institute for Legal Reform* claimed that the difference in the legal environment between the U.S. and other countries contributed to an increase in liability costs of 0.81% of the GDP. To be clear, the U.S. GDP in 2016 was $18.57 trillion, 1.66% of it is $308 billion. The 0.81% attributed to the difference in legal environment (of which the number of lawyers per capita is a significant factor) represents $150 billion by itself… annually.

Divided by the number of U.S. Residents, this constitutes $956 of civil litigation spending per capita per year. To put this number in perspective, there are 28 countries in the world whose GDP per capita is lower than that (sources: CIA,[121] World Bank[122]).

And it gets worse. According to the global advisory, broking, and solutions company, Willis Towers Watson, the growth in civil litigation costs in the U.S. grew between 1951 and 2010 in an average rate of 8.7% annually. In the same period, the U.S. GDP grew only 6.7% annually on average.[123] While this annual difference seems small, when compounded over the entire 60-year period, the GDP grew 48 times, while litigation costs grew 148 times. More than three times faster. At this rate, by 2025, the U.S. will spend a trillion dollars on civil litigation. In 2008, the cost of medical liability alone in the U.S. reached 2.4% (or $55.6 billion) of the overall annual health care spending.[124]

A 2015 report by Norton Rose Fulbright[125] showed that the U.S. leads the world in a few additional categories:

- The highest percentage of litigation with value of more than $10 million per case (25% compared to 19% average);
- The lowest percentage of litigation with value of less than $500,000 (21% compared to 36% average);

- The fastest *growth* in litigation spending (25% of cases over $10 million in 2014, up from 17% two years earlier, 70% cases over $1 million in 2014, up from 52% in 2012); *and*

- The percentage of class actions brought against companies (37% compared to 16% in the UK, 10% in Canada, and 6% in Australia).

As the number of lawyers increased in the U.S., so did the number of lawsuits. Between 1993 and 2002 the number of civil lawsuits increased 12% to over 16 million cases filed in 2002. Trial lawyers earned an estimated $40 billion that year. The largest increase in lawsuits was in healthcare. As a result, 79% of physicians reported that they ordered more tests than they would have otherwise based upon their professional judgement. The *American Medical Association* listed 21 states as being in a "medical liability crisis." As many as 71,000 drug lawsuits were filed in federal courts since 2001, outnumbering suits over asbestos, tobacco, and auto safety. As many as 45% of U.S. hospitals reported that the liability crisis caused a loss of physicians and reduced coverage in Emergency Rooms.[126]

The number of ADA (*Americans with Disabilities Act*) Title II lawsuits rose 143% from 2013 (2,722 lawsuits) to 2016 (6,601 lawsuits); 250 of those suits in 2016 were over allegedly inaccessible websites or mobile apps. Three plaintiffs that same year filed more than 200 lawsuits each, and 12 plaintiffs filed more than 100 lawsuits each. An attempt to reduce the number of such lawsuits through proposing the *ADA Education and Reform Act* in 2016 failed.[127]

As the numbers show, we have, unfortunately, a litigious culture. But we couldn't stop here without giving a few examples. As before, we offer these examples without any commentary.

Warning, content may be hot!

On February 1992, 79-year-old Stella Liebeck bought a cup of coffee at a drive-thru *McDonalds*. As she picked up the hot beverage, she spilled it over her legs, accidentally, and suffered third-degree burns. The court awarded her $200,000 in damages initially. It was later reduced to $160,000 because the jury attributed 20% of the fault to her. The court also awarded $2.7 million in punitive damages.[128]

Reserved parking

On August 2017, Christi Bowmer drove her BMW inside an Austin, Texas parking garage. Looking for parking, she reached the seventh floor of the garage. There, as she started parking her car, her foot slipped from the brake pedal and landed on the accelerator pedal. The car accelerated into the edge cable barrier, which was not strong enough to stop it. The car broke through the barrier and flew down seven stories, to land on its top. Ms. Bowmer survived the fall, and later sued the parking garage operator for $1 million for "physical injuries, physical pain, physical impairment, disfigurement, mental anguish and medical expenses." The lawsuit included her husband, who was not in the car, for damages from the crash, including "mental anguish and lost earnings."[129]

Satisfaction guaranteed

On May 3, 2005, former D.C. Judge Roy L. Pearson Jr. left his pants with the local dry cleaner. When he came back to pick them up two days later, he claimed that these were not his pants, despite the fact that the cleaners' records, tags, and receipt indicated that they were. He went on to file a lawsuit for more than $67 million against the cleaners, which he later reduced to $54 million just prior to trial. The basis for the lawsuit was, other than the loss of the pants, that the sign posted outside advertised "Satisfaction Guaranteed," which he claimed was misleading. He lost the case, as well as several appeals and appeal requests after that. During the litigation, he refused multiple settlement offers by the dry cleaners.[130] We will return to the facts of this case later.

A litigious society

This increasingly litigious environment we live in forces organizations that have authority over our lives (our employers, schools, etc.) and deep pockets to do everything they can to avoid litigation. In the process, they force policies, regulations, and Political Correctness upon us. They simply don't want to get sued.

But why are we such a litigious society? There are two main reasons for that: the way the American legal system operates and the disproportional growth in the number of lawyers in the U.S.

***

We could use this opportunity to make lawyer jokes, but we won't. Lawyers have feelings, too. And one of us does hold a law degree…

But, do we really have too many lawyers? Different sources claim that between 70% and 80% of the world's lawyers live in the U.S.[131] In 2016, there were just over 1.3 million lawyers practicing in the U.S. That's 40.3 lawyers per 10,000 residents (1 lawyer per 248 residents). The state with the highest ratio is New York, with 88.7 lawyers per 10,000 residents (1 in 113). And if you thought that Washington D.C. is the state with the highest ratio—you were wrong. Washington D.C. is not a state... If we include the 52,711 lawyers active in D.C. in 2016, D.C. is leading with a whopping 778.8 lawyers per 10,000 residents, or 1 in 13![132]

We studied the population growth in the U.S. between 1900 and 2015, as reported by the U.S. Census Bureau. During that period, the U.S. population grew from 76.2 million to 320.9 million, or 321%.[133,134] We then studied the *American Bar Association* national lawyer population survey results between 1878 and 2017, and correlated the two. In the same period, the number of lawyers grew from 114,460 in 1900 to 1,300,705 in 2015, or 1,035%![135] In other words, the lawyer population in the U.S. grew more than 3 times faster than the general U.S. population did. While lawyers represented 0.15% of the population in 1900, they represented 0.41% of the population in 2015.

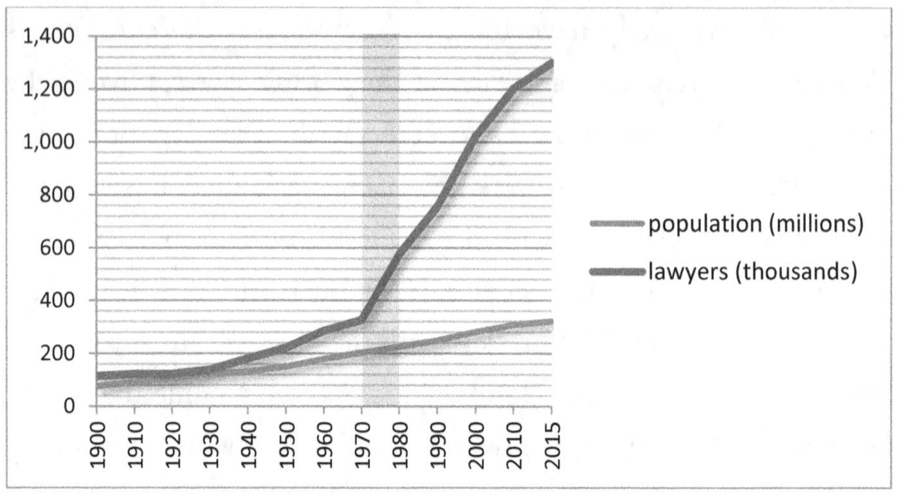

Figure 24: Population and lawyers' growth

It's easy to say that we simply have too many lawyers and leave it at that, but the chart above reveals something else. You can see that between 1900 and 1930 (the Great Depression) the percentage of lawyers as part of the general population declined. Lawyer population growth was only 35% of the general population growth. In 1930 only 0.11% of the population was lawyers.

If we stretch the data range to between 1900 and 1970, the growth in number of lawyers was relatively similar to the growth in overall U.S. population. While the overall number of people in the U.S. grew 167%, the number of lawyers grew 185% in the same period. In the 1960s and 1970s, the percentage of lawyers as part of general population reached roughly the same levels it had in 1900, 0.16%. The ratio of the growth in the number of U.S. lawyers to the growth in general U.S. population was only 1.1 to 1.

However, something happened in the turn of the 1970s, as the growth in the number of lawyers started accelerating faster. Between 1970 and 2015, while the general U.S. population grew 58%, the U.S. lawyer population grew 298%, or 5.14 times faster than the general population growth, and reached a level of 0.41% of the U.S. population. In other words, in 2015, one in every 244 men, women, and children was a lawyer (1 in 248 by 2016).

The fastest growing decade for lawyers was the 1970s (the gray area on the chart). In a single decade, the number of American lawyers increased almost 76%, outpacing population growth by a ratio of 7-to-1.

What happened in the 1970s? We will answer this question in the next chapter. For now, we will reveal another interesting fact that could explain some of the partisan polarization in our legislative branch. While 0.41% of the U.S. Population (0.6% of adults) is lawyers, 41% of the 113th Congress (2013) was made of lawyers. In other words—members of Congress are 68 times more likely to have practiced law than the general U.S. adult population.[136]

The Day that Changed our Culture

To find the reason for the sudden disproportionate growth in the number of lawyers in the 1970s, we turned to the enrollment numbers in American law schools.[137] This data was available to us by year, and not only by decade. The first chart shows the first year law school enrollment numbers.

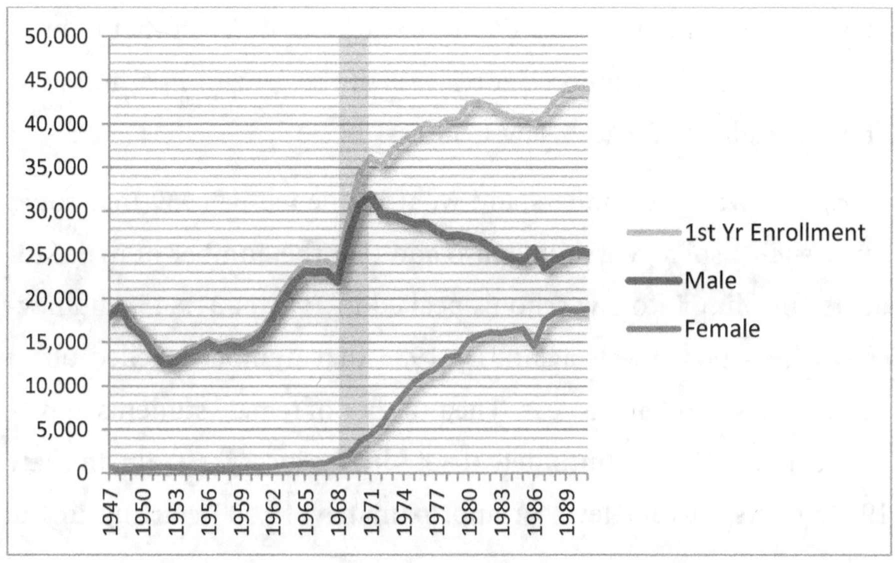

Figure 25: Law school enrollment

Note that before 1963, the first year enrollment numbers never exceeded 20,000 per year. While it was growing consistently from 1959 to 1965 (60% in those 6 years, or 8.2% every year), it leveled off in 1965, and even declined mildly from 1965 to 1968.

Also, note that the number of female student first year law school enrollments had almost no effect on the total number of first year enrollment before 1967. In fact, 1965 was the first year that saw the number of female students enrolling into law schools surpass 1,000 (nationwide). For comparison, the number of male students applying to law schools that year was over 23,000.

But that is not the elephant in the room. One thing that jumps out at you from that chart is the sudden growth in the number of male student first year law school admissions starting in 1969. In a span of only three years (1968 to 1971, the gray area in the chart) that number jumped from 21,910 to 31,845, or 45%. Of that jump, a single year, 1969, accounted for 23.3% of the growth in admissions of male students into U.S. law schools.

Before we try to understand what happened in 1969 that could cause such a spike, we should also add that the number of male students enrolling into law schools peaked in 1971 at 31,845, and never reached those levels again. By 1983 that number levelled off at about 25,000 students a year. The number of female students applying to law schools continued to gradually increase from the late 1960s to its current level of approximately 19,000 starting in the 1980s.

As a result, while the number of male students applying to law schools declined since 1971, the total enrollment numbers increased until they reached a steady level of 40,000 to 45,000 new law students every year. The number of law schools had to catch up with that increase in the number of student applications. Due to the time it takes to build schools, the growth in the number of schools was somewhat dampened. The biggest single year growth between 1946 and 2011 was, as expected, in 1969. Six new law schools were launched that year (a 4.35% increase).

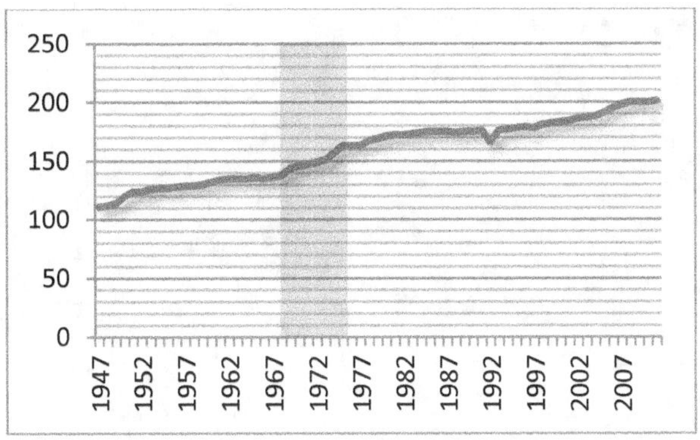

Figure 26: Total number of U.S. law schools

However, as the number of law schools reached their steady level of 170 to 202, they remained capable of supporting that high number of students. Between 2008 and 2016, the number of applicants into law schools dropped between 20.6% (for the top 14 schools) to 52.3% for the rest. And what do you do when demand goes down? You lower the admission requirements to keep those enrollment numbers up.[138] The average acceptance rate increased from 31.5% in 2008 to 55% in 2014, and 52% in 2016, so those seats built to meet the demand in the 1970s will be filled.[139] Supply and Demand in all of its glory.

One thing is clear; the 1969 spike in U.S. law school enrollment had a snowball effect on the continuous disproportionate growth in the number of lawyers that we see today.

***

A review of the overall college enrollment numbers[140] shows a steady growth, even throughout the Vietnam War.

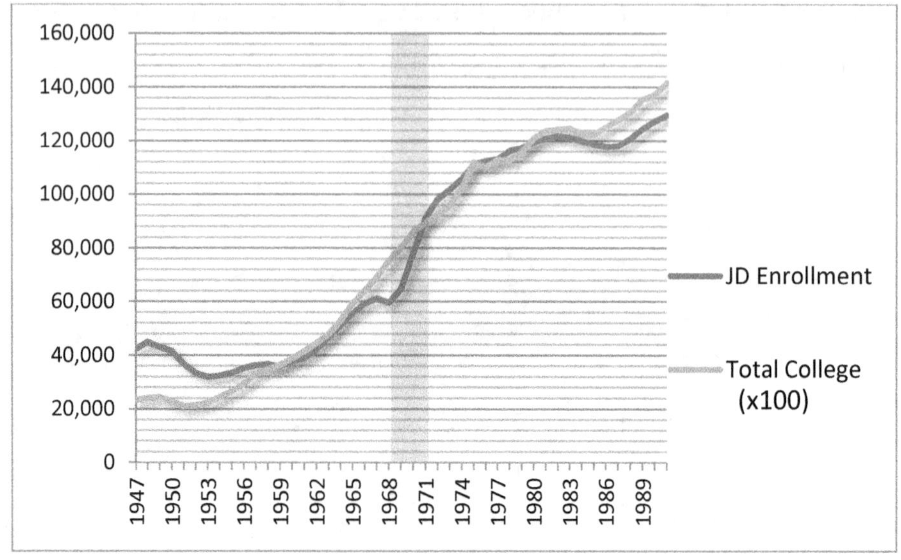

Figure 27: Law school enrollment

While law students represented 0.79% of all college students in 1968, this rate jumped to 1.06% by 1972. Between 1969 and 1972, 89,617 men were enrolled (not only first year) in law schools, and by 1973 this number climbed to 119,240.

The 60s

So what happened in the 1960s?[141] The following is a list of some of the major events that took place during that decade.

1960: John F. Kennedy (D) defeats Richard Nixon (R) to become the 35th President of the United States. He was the second youngest person to be elected into that office.

1961: Soviet Cosmonaut Yuri Gagarin becomes the first person in space. The result, President Kennedy makes his famous Rice University speech calling to put the first American on the moon before the end of the century.

1961: The CIA's Bay of Pigs invasion of Cuba in an attempt to overthrow Fidel Castro fails.

1961: The Peace Corps is created.

1962: The Cuban Missile Crisis that almost caused the beginning of World War III, which would have been a nuclear war with devastating consequences.

1962: The Beetles release their first song and album.

1962: James Meredith becomes the first African-American student enrolled at the University of Mississippi.

1962: Sam Walton opens the first Walmart store in Arkansas.

1963: President Kennedy is assassinated in Dallas, Texas, fueling multiple conspiracy theories, many of which suggest that the U.S. government itself was involved in killing the beloved President.

1963: Dr. Martin Luther King, Jr. gives his passionate "I have a Dream" speech that sparks the civil rights movement.

1964: President Lyndon B. Johnson (D) signs the *Civil Rights Act of 1964* into law.

1964: Sidney Poitier becomes the first African-American actor to win an Oscar for Best Actor.

1965: LBJ signs the *Voting Rights Act* into law.

1965: Dr. Martin Luther King, Jr. leads the civil rights march from Selma to Montgomery, Alabama.

1966: Indira Gandhi becomes the first female prime minister of India.

1967: Thurgood Marshall becomes the first African-American to be appointed to the U.S. Supreme Court.

1968: Dr. Martin Luther King, Jr. is assassinated.

1969: The *Civil Rights Act of 1968* is signed into law by President Johnson.

1969: Apollo 11 puts a man on the moon (and a U.S. flag).

1969: The Woodstock music festival in New York.

The 1960s signify the birth of the *Consciousness Movement* (also known as the *Black Consciousness Movement*). In his book, *The Generational Imperative*,[142] author Chuck Underwood quotes: "[America] remakes itself in fairer terms, beginning the process of righting our wrongs." He further described several movements that attempted to right those wrongs:

- The Civil Rights Movement (MLK, Malcolm X, Chavez, Means);
- The Feminist Movement (Gloria Steinem);
- The Ecology Movement;
- The War Protest Movement;
- The Sexual Revolution; *and*
- The Drug Revolution

The last two were very apparent during the Woodstock Concert in New York in August of 1969.

The unrest building in the late 1960s was also fueled by the promise made by President Johnson to reduce the number of American soldiers in Vietnam and, instead, increased it, and by the fact that high-school graduates were about to get drafted, yet could not vote to make an impact.

All those movements and events shifted the American society from its industrialized-focus to a more liberal, social focus.

***

So, what happened in 1969? Why such a huge spike in male student enrollment that year?

To answer this question, we turned again to history. The biggest event affecting the U.S. in the late 1960s and early 1970s was happening somewhere in East Asia. The U.S. was involved in the Vietnam War. In order to understand the connection to the enrollment numbers, we ask you to put yourself in the shoes of a high school student graduating between 1963 and 1969.

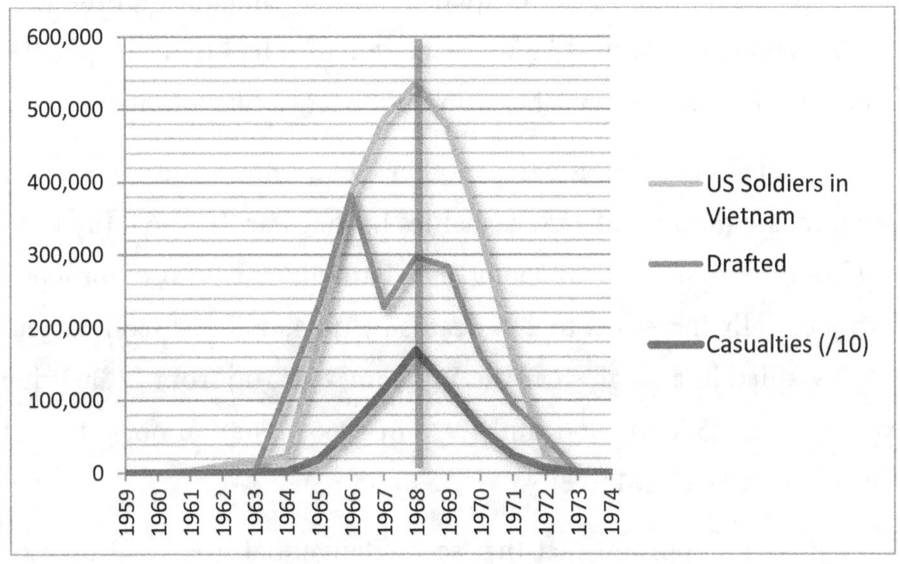

Figure 28: U.S. involvement in Vietnam

As the chart above shows, the U.S. involvement in Vietnam was at its peak in 1968. The level of U.S. troops in Vietnam reached 536,100,[143] up from 23,300 only four years earlier, in 1964. There is absolutely no way that you didn't know quite a few people who went to Vietnam. The majority (75%) of the U.S. force in Vietnam was made of volunteers. Even though only 25% (648,500) of the

U.S. force in Vietnam was made of draftees, the numbers are still staggering, and draftees accounted for 30.4% (17,725) of combat deaths in Vietnam.[144] While 112,356 men were drafted in 1964, those numbers rose to 382,010 in 1966 and 296,406 in 1968. The level of drafted U.S. soldiers held steady at 283,586 in 1969. Remember that while the levels were steady, soldiers who were killed, injured, captured as POWs, were missing, or simply returned home after finishing their tour of duty, had to be replaced by new soldiers, some of which were drafted. Again, as much as you had to know people who served in Vietnam, you also had to know people who were *drafted* to serve there, and not necessarily volunteered.

As a high-school graduate, another trend caused you even more anxiety: the number of U.S. casualties in that war. In 1960, the U.S. suffered the first 5 casualties in the Vietnam War. Those numbers exponentially increased to 216 deaths in 1964, and in 1968 reached 16,899 killed in a single year the Vietnam War (up from 11,363 the year before, 6,350 in 1966, and 1,928 in 1965). That number started declining in 1969 to 11,780.[145]

Another important fact that seems tangential to all of this was that there was no television during World War II. The use of television started at the same time as the beginning of the Korean War, but less than 4 million U.S. households owned one. Those numbers rose dramatically, until in 1969, there were almost 60 million U.S. households with a TV, of which two-thirds were in color.[146] You could not avoid seeing the images from Vietnam or the images of those coffins unloaded from planes coming back to U.S. soil.

In fact, the numbers of U.S. soldiers in Vietnam, young men being drafted, and U.S. soldiers killed in Vietnam started declining after 1968, and by 1973, the war was over. U.S. troops came home, draftees were discharged from military service, and the casualties stopped. But in 1969 you had no way of knowing that the war would be over in four years. Nobody did. If you looked at the trends leading to 1968, you would assume that the dotted lines are what those numbers would be in 1969 and beyond. You would expect the number of U.S. soldiers in Vietnam to exceed 650,000 in 1970, and that the number of casualties would exceed 26,000 that year.

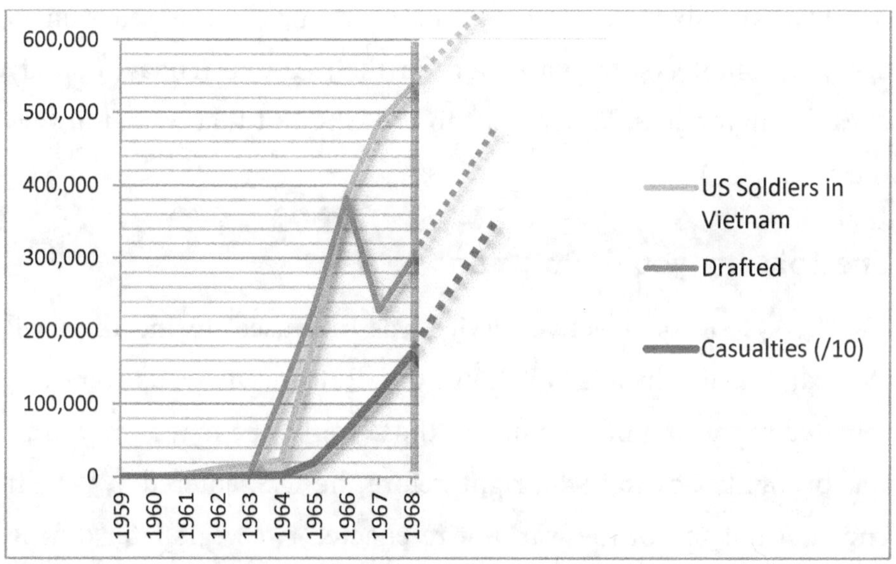

Figure 29: What it looked like in 1969

Even if you knew those numbers would start declining in 1970, four years is still a long time to serve in the Vietnam War, and maybe even be killed.

***

Some countries in the world don't have a military force at all. Those are mostly small countries that would not be able to defend themselves on their own, and have to rely on much stronger allies and treaties. There are 32 counties in which military service is mandatory. Those include Israel, Vietnam, Korea (South and North) and Cuba, among others. If you live in a country with mandatory military service, you know it is coming. In Israel, you join the military immediately after your high-school graduation. Although you have the option to defer your service until after you obtained a college degree, the service will be waiting for you. It is highly predictable and anything but uncertain. The U.S. relies on an army of volunteers, who are paid for their service. Today, nobody goes through a mandatory draft in the U.S. But that wasn't always the case.

The lottery you didn't want to win

The system of selective service was first used during the Civil War, and again during WWI, but the draft mechanisms were terminated at the end of each one of those wars. The mandatory draft was brought back in 1940, right before the U.S. entered WWII. It ended at the end of the war, but re-enacted two years later during the Cold War. The next time it would expire would be in 1973, at the end of the Vietnam War.[147] More than 2.8 million men were inducted through the draft in WWI, 10.1 million in WWII, 1.5 million during the Korean War, and 1.9 million during the Vietnam War. The last man inducted entered service on Jun 30, 1973.[148]

To make the mandatory draft process equitable, a lottery system was first implemented in 1942. The second time was on December 1st, 1969, during the height of the Vietnam War. On November 26, 1969, President Richard Nixon signed *Executive Order 11497*, amending the selective service regulations to prescribe random selection, through a lottery, and setting the order and priority of calling men to service.[149]

In a very ceremonial event (in a very unceremonious setting), Congressman Alexander Pirnie (R-NY) of the *House Armed Services Committee* pulled the first of 366 blue capsules from a drum that was tumbled in order to shuffle those capsules. He opened the first capsule and read the date: September 14.[150] If you were born on September 14 between the years 1944 and 1950 (so you would have been at least 18 years old, but not yet 26 on January 1, 1970) you were going to be the first to be drafted. You may have just seen your death warrant being signed. And so the following capsules were pulled, and the dates inside them assigned to the following numbers, in sequence, until the last capsule was drawn, holding the date June 8. That date was assigned the number 366.

The 1969 draft lottery caused the largest number of men to be drafted. The highest number ever called for a physical exam was 215. The highest number processed was 195 for the 1969 lottery. If you were born between 1944 and 1950, and your date was assigned to a number higher than 195, you were safe. The result was the following table.

	Jan	Feb	Mar	Apr	May	Jun	Jul	Aug	Sep	Oct	Nov	Dec
1	305	86	108	32	330	249	93	111	225	359	19	129
2	159	144	29	271	298	228	350	45	161	125	34	328
3	251	297	267	83	40	301	115	261	49	244	348	157
4	215	210	275	81	276	20	279	145	232	202	266	165
5	101	214	293	269	364	28	188	54	82	24	310	56
6	224	347	139	253	155	110	327	114	6	87	76	10
7	306	91	122	147	35	85	50	168	8	234	51	12
8	199	181	213	312	321	366	13	48	184	283	97	105
9	194	338	317	219	197	335	277	106	263	342	80	43
10	325	216	323	218	65	206	284	21	71	220	282	41
11	329	150	136	14	37	134	248	324	158	237	46	39
12	221	68	300	346	133	272	15	142	242	72	66	314
13	318	152	259	124	295	69	42	307	175	138	126	163
14	238	4	354	231	178	356	331	198	1	294	127	26
15	17	89	169	273	130	180	322	102	113	171	131	320
16	121	212	166	148	55	274	120	44	207	254	107	96
17	235	189	33	260	112	73	98	154	255	288	143	304
18	140	292	332	90	278	341	190	141	246	5	146	128
19	58	25	200	336	75	104	227	311	177	241	203	240
20	280	302	239	345	183	360	187	344	63	192	185	135
21	186	363	334	62	250	60	27	291	204	243	156	70
22	337	290	265	316	326	247	153	339	160	117	9	53
23	118	57	256	252	319	109	172	116	119	201	182	162
24	59	236	258	2	31	358	23	36	195	196	230	95
25	52	179	343	351	361	137	67	286	149	176	132	84
26	92	365	170	340	357	22	303	245	18	7	309	173
27	355	205	268	74	296	64	289	352	233	264	47	78
28	77	299	223	262	308	222	88	167	257	94	281	123
29	349	285	362	191	226	353	270	61	151	229	99	16
30	164	–	217	208	103	209	287	333	315	38	174	3
31	211	–	30	–	313	–	193	11	–	79	–	100

Figure 30: The 1969 draft lottery

Based on the short interviews we conducted with men who were eligible to be drafted in the 1969 lottery, we understand that looking at the draft lottery table might bring back stressful memories. Nevertheless, it is important that others understand what you experienced.

Based on your date of birth, you would find your draft number in this table. If you were born on January 26th, your lottery number would have been 92 (look at the January column and 26th row). Being born on September 14th meant that you would be the first to be called into service in Vietnam. On the other hand, if you were fortunate enough to be born on June 8th, you knew that you would be the last to be called into service. Following your date of birth, a second number was drawn for your last name, in case there was no need for all who were born on a certain date.[151]

The 1969 lottery had a more significant impact than similar draft lotteries that followed in each of the next six years. The 1970 lottery applied only to those born in 1951. The 1971 lottery applied only to those born in 1952, and so on. The level of U.S. troops in Vietnam started declining after 1969, so fewer draftees were needed. However, the 1969 lottery applied to those born between 1944 and 1950, estimated at 850,000 men. It affected a much larger size population and was done during the peak of the number of U.S. troops in Vietnam.[152]

The psychological effect of the draft lottery

The draft lottery had a tremendous impact on people's lives, especially those subject to it.[153] If you don't believe us, find a man born between 1944 and 1950. That man would have been subject to the draft lottery on December 1, 1969. Without giving him any background, ask him a simple question: "what was your lottery number?" We asked many men of that age and found that, even though it happened 48 years ago, they clearly remember their number, and the evening in which it was drawn. We asked someone to send a text to a man he knew that was born in that timeframe. All the text included was: "What was your lottery number?" Nothing else. No explanation or background. It wasn't a minute later and the response came back: "27." In the following text, he added: "Everyone knows their lottery number. It was actually a pretty scary time. We watched that war on television and we were all worried." To get a sense of the feelings you might have experienced on the night of December 1, 1969, you could watch the CBS broadcast of that event.[154] Can you imagine watching that broadcast and every time a capsule is opened, you hope it didn't contain your birth date?

Why did the draft lottery have such a big impact on people's lives? Uncertainty is a very powerful emotion. We hate uncertainty. Do you like the uncertainty of the weather? Do you like financial uncertainty? Not knowing if you would be able to provide for yourself and your family tomorrow? How about the uncertainty of possibly getting killed in Vietnam and joining the 48,732 men your age who returned home in a casket covered with the American flag between the beginning of the war and December 1969?

Some say that it was even worse for those with numbers in the middle. If you had a high number, you were safe. If you had a low number, you knew you were going to war. If you drew a number in the middle, you had to live with the profound uncertainty and possibility of disrupting your life for years. And you know how much you like that kind of uncertainty.[155]

The number drawn in the 1969 lottery had an impact on political affiliation, too. A study conducted by *Columbia University* in 2010 showed that the probability of draft-age men to vote for President Nixon (who signed the draft lottery into law in 1969) was 34% for those who had lottery number 1, who were certain to be drafted and sent to Vietnam, and 74% for those with lottery number 366, who were highly unlikely to be drafted. For those who identified as strong Republicans in 1965, if they drew number 1 in the lottery, there was only a 50% probability that they would keep their party affiliation, but 76% if they drew number 366. Even for those identified as strong Democrats, the probability of them changing parties increased as their draft number was higher.[156]

Finally, the Federal Reserve Bank found, in a report published in 2015, that there was a strong correlation between being eligible for the Vietnam draft and lower earning potential of their sons, many years later.[157] Parents model how to deal with stress and kids are sponges that absorb those responses. A dad, who had suffered the trauma associated with the Vietnam draft, whether or not he went, may have unintentionally influenced his son to perceive the world in a negative way.

PTSD and the draft

Post-Traumatic Stress Disorder (PTSD) is a clinically proven disorder on both a psychological and physiological level. We emphasize "clinically proven" because for decades before it was considered a soldier's cowardly way of getting out of the service during a war. One of the key criteria to be diagnosed with PTSD is that the person must have either been in a perceived life-threatening situation or they witnessed one. Being called up for the draft could be perceived as a life threatening situation. Fear is a very powerful emotion that does alter the human brain and body. When a trauma occurs, research has shown that the structures of the lower brain, or hind-brain, are altered; the Hippocampus and Amygdala change in size due to the result of trauma.

Imagine that you are an 18-year-old man in 1969. You just graduated from high school and think that the whole world is ahead of you, getting a job, meeting your future wife, getting married buying a house, a car, and having 2.5 kids.

Then one night, you are watching birthdates being read aloud and placed on a large board with other birthdates. With each date being pulled out of the capsule, your heart freezes with dread, your adrenaline rises, your thoughts race, concentration is shot, and you unknowingly hold your breath. You are so grateful that you were not born on September 14. Even after a number is called and it isn't yours, you have just enough time to take a quick breath before the next one is called. The anxiety may subside for a short period of time, but it is close at hand, knowing that it is a matter of time before the next set of numbers are called… will it be yours? Then, you get your draft card in the mail... a rude, sobering reality comes crashing into your world. There may be a passing thought that at least you are no longer in the limbo state of waiting.

A new reality is formed, one of rows of caskets, hearses driving down the street, buddies being shot as they get off the plane, and your classmates shouting "baby killer" to anyone in a uniform. The images seen on TV are the ones that you keep replaying in your head… over and over again. How can you make plans for your future when you aren't sure that you will have one? Each graphic image on a news-reel or in a magazine becomes seared into your head as you think "that could be me."

Given that state of anxiety for, perhaps, years of a young man's life, it is understandable how the association with that lottery number and fear are intricately linked and the number seared into his memory for decades. Even now, when asked about the number, a similar physiological response, although a lessened one, may still take place.

No doubt, the psychological consequences of the Vietnam draft and the 1969 draft lottery were more significant than anyone could have imagined.

Avoiding the draft

In 1969, you belonged to one of three groups.[158] The first group was made of people who were legally and legitimately *ineligible* to serve. That group included *true* conscientious objectors (on the basis of religion and the like), those who had a *real* medical or psychological condition preventing them from serving, those holding essential civilian jobs, men with children, homosexuals, or women. Approximately 11,000 American women served in Vietnam during the war, but nearly all of them were volunteers, with 90% of them as serving as nurses.[159]

The second group included those who evaded the draft illegally. Those who faked a health or psychological condition, lied about their status, burned their draft notice, or fled to Canada (or any other country, for that matter). That was an illegal way to avoid the draft, and if and when you were caught, you could be sentenced to serve prison time.

If you didn't illegally avoid the draft or had a valid condition preventing you from serving, then you belonged to the third group—those who were eligible to serve. Their classification was known as 1-A. Many of those were drafted and sent to Vietnam. Many of them were killed in action there. If you were eligible to be drafted, there could only be three reasons why you would still be able to avoid the draft. The first was to have a high-lottery number. That was not up to you, and it was the reason that there were such high stakes that night in December 1969. Alternatively, you could enlist voluntarily. Many, eager to serve their country, enlisted and went before they were drafted; 75% of the American soldiers in Vietnam were volunteers. Some chose "safer" branches of the U.S. military, such as the Coast Guard, where they would not be sent to war. There was only one other deferment from the draft for those eligible to serve. It was known as the 2-S deferment—going to college.[160]

***

So, while the December 1, 1969 draft lottery may have been a triggering event, it was fueled by a social transformation in American society, combined with anti-government and anti-war pressures, causing the trigger to push in the direction of law schools, more than any other kind of college. For this book, we interviewed men who graduated from high school prior to the December 1969 lottery. We found several interesting insights. One was that not all 18-year-olds were as afraid to fight in Vietnam as much as their families were. That's understandable. In many cases, the parents were the ones who did their best to get their boys into college and use the education deferment, and not the boys themselves. We also found that many chose to volunteer to any of the U.S. military branches ahead of the draft (and the lottery), as they wanted to be more in control of their future. Finally, we found an almost overwhelming correlation: those who were subject to the draft and the draft lottery remember their lottery number without hesitation, almost 50 years later, as if the lottery happened yesterday. Those who took other routes (whether college, Canada, or even volunteered into the U.S. Armed Forces without waiting to be drafted) or were not subject to the draft lottery didn't remember that number. This correlation speaks volumes to the psychological impact that the lottery had on them.

***

We have now demonstrated an undisputable link between the 1969 Draft Lottery and the litigious culture and Political Correctness we have today. It goes through the fear and uncertainty of being drafted to the Vietnam War, through using the college deferment to get out of the draft, going to law school, where the number of students admitted every year doubled in just a few years to new steady levels, to the continuous increase in the number of lawyers per capita in the U.S. that started in the 1970s, to suing over anything, to forcing people to be Politically Correct to avoid those lawsuits.

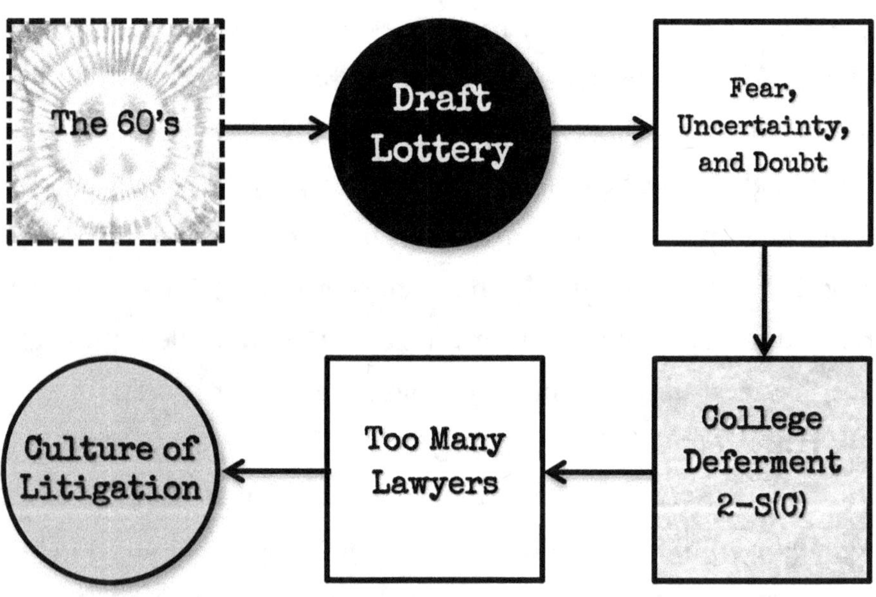

Figure 31: The day that changed American culture

There is another, even more direct link between the mandatory Vietnam draft and Political Correctness, proposed by the *Accuracy in Academia* organization. In their February 2000 essay about the origins of Political Correctness,[161] they claimed that the student rebellion in the mid-1960s, driven largely by the resistance to the draft and the Vietnam War, needed some kind of ideology to support it. It couldn't just be "Hell no, we won't go," and Political Correctness gave them that ideological foundation they needed.

The anger and disillusionment following President Johnson's *Gulf of Tonkin* resolution and escalation of the U.S. military presence in Vietnam in 1965 sparked a 20,000-student demonstration in Washington D.C. on April 17, 1965, led by the *Students for Democratic Society* (SDS) movement in the *University of Michigan*. One of the march organizers, Paul Booth, said that

> we're really not just a peace group. We are working on domestic problems—civil rights, poverty, [and] university reform. We feel passionately and angrily about things in America, and we feel that a war in Asia will destroy what we're trying to do here.

By the summer of that year, protests erupted in colleges all over the U.S. The focus of the SDS movement shifted to specifically objecting the draft.[162]

***

But there is yet another reason why we have a culture of litigation. This one is not less sinister, but unlike the Vietnam draft lottery—this one is intentional.

Litigation-Backed Securities

In your first week of the micro-economics class you learn about supply and demand. What you learn is that when demand stays the same, yet supply increases; prices must go down to the new equilibrium point where supply meets demand. For example, if the number of cars manufactured in a certain economy exceeds the demand for new cars, car manufacturers would have to lower prices to compete over the customers who were planning to buy cars.

In our case, we assume that the demand for lawyers and lawsuits is not increasing, yet the supply of lawyers increases in a disproportionate way. The result must be that the hourly rates would have declined. Did they?

This disproportionate increase in the number of lawyers defies the basic economics law of supply and demand. In general, when the supply (number of lawyers) increases, considering no change in the demand for those services, the price (attorney fees) should decline. However, the *2017 Legal Trends Report*[163] indicated the opposite. Between 2012 and 2017 (the period covered in that report), the lawyer average billing rate increased from $229 to $260, an increase of $31, or 13.5%. However, the *Consumer Price Index* (CPI) increased only 6.45% in that time.[164] Less than half of the increase in attorney fees!

It should be noted that, according to the *2017 Legal Trends Report*, 86% of the legal fees are collected. Only 14% of the bills go uncollected. This fact will play a role two chapters down the road. Finally, the report also reveals that the most profitable cases are the *Personal Injury* cases.

In a 2016 article,[165] the Wall Street Journal indicated that, for the first time, law firms charged hourly rates in excess of $1,500 per hour. In fact, since the 2008 economic downturn, law firms have raised their rates between 3% and 4% every year. The *American Bar Association* published the 2015 hourly rate fact sheet,[166] in which they indicated that in only two years, between 2013 and 2015, the median hourly rate for full-time lawyers increased by 7.4%, the hourly rate for women attorneys increased by 9.6%, the rates for male attorneys increased by 11.3% (there's a lawsuit waiting to happen right there…), the rates for racial minority attorneys increased by 14.7%, the rates for white attorney increased by 6.1%, the rates for attorneys in metropolitan regions increased 8.2%, for non-metropolitan attorneys by 20.6%, and for out of state/country by 9.7%. In only two years.

Doesn't that fly in the face of the basic supply and demand law? If the supply (number of attorneys) continues to grow disproportionately relative to the general population, why are the hourly rates increasing and not decreasing? The only thing that could explain that is if the demand continues to grow, even faster than the number of lawyers. But what would make the demand continue to grow?

✳✳✳

The movie *The Big Short*, describing the 2008 housing market crash, is an eye-opener. Understanding how investors and bankers found a way to create *mortgage-based securities* and profit from those was interesting, to say the least. The American people are very creative. Where there is an opportunity to make money—we find it. Of course, the outcome of investing in mortgage-backed securities was that brokers stopped checking the ability of sub-prime borrowers to pay back their debt because, as was portrayed in the movie: "if I write a loan on Friday afternoon, big bank is going to buy it by Monday lunch." This bubble was bound to burst, and in 2008 it did.

But it isn't only mortgage-backed securities that we invest in. In fact, right before the housing market and the mortgage-backed securities market began to collapse, investment banks, such as *Goldman Sachs*, began to place large negative bets ("shorts"), and practically bet against their clients. In December 2006, Goldman Sachs changed their stance on the mortgage market from positive to negative, but without disclosing it publicly; during that time they were still selling mortgage-backed securities to their clients.[167] One of the big "winners" of the sub-prime mortgage market collapse was a trader by the name John Paulson, whose firm made $15 billion in 2007 by shorting the subprime mortgage securities market. Paulson himself earned $4 billion for those trades,[168] while many Americans lost their life savings and their homes.

While investment tools were originally created to provide funding for companies to *grow*, allowing investors to benefit from such growth, new investment tools were created that caused the opposite. *Short Selling,* for example, is "the sale of a security that is not owned by the seller or that the seller has borrowed. Short selling is motivated by the belief that a security's price will decline, enabling it to be bought back at a lower price to make a profit."[169] In other words, short selling allows an investor to benefit from the *decline* of a company, the market, or the economy.

Hedge fund firms invest using multiple strategies, including non-orthodox ones. They are very aggressive and face fewer regulations than mutual funds and other investment vehicles.[170] Perhaps the strongest indication of our willingness to invest in anything is the growth in the hedge fund industry. Between 2000 and 2014, the number of hedge funds operating in North America grew from 500 to 1,300 (160%), while the amount of money managed by those funds grew from $1.1 trillion to $5.7 trillion (418%).[171]

In 2009, a new type of currency was invented: cryptocurrency. Specifically, Bitcoin. A discussion of this new type of currency is beyond the scope of our book, but the *trading* in Bitcoin is not. On July 19, 2010, one Bitcoin was worth $0.06. As we entered 2017, the value of one Bitcoin soared to exceed $1,000. Within a year, right before the end of 2017, one Bitcoin was worth $19,343.[172] It didn't take long to "securitize" Bitcoins, and on December 10, 2017, the Chicago Board Options Exchange (CBOE)[173] Futures Exchange began trading in Bitcoin futures.[174] Those surged more than 19% during the first day of trading, triggering two trading halts Sunday night due to excessive price gains.[175] By January 11, 2018, one month after the beginning of trading, Bitcoin price declined to

$13,287, and at the time of writing this paragraph on January 16, Bitcoin futures dropped below $11,000, and by the time we started editing this book on April 1st, it traded at $6,759. Quite the roller-coaster ride. Securities regulator Joseph Borg says that the Bitcoin mania caused people to take mortgages on their homes just to be able to "get in on the action."[176]

***

The aforementioned stories say more about us than our pure desire to invest. They say that we are greedy. We abandon the ethical bar and as long as it is not illegal, we will invest in it. We are the center of the universe, and it doesn't matter who gets hurt, if we can benefit. In fact, we invest and benefit even from other people's failure.

Furthermore, incentives drive behaviors. We behave in a way that will maximize our incentive. If maximizing the incentives of a hedge fund manager means that they should avoid checking the borrowers' ability to pay off their mortgages, so be it! If maximizing incentives means they need to bet against their own clients' investments—bring it on! We will do whatever it takes to get those incentives. Because incentives drive behaviors.

And so, as creative investors, we constantly look for alternative investment channels, regardless of the consequences, and the circumstances had just presented us with a new one.

***

In the American legal system, every party is responsible for its own legal fees, irrespective of the type of case. However, this rule can be modified by statute or by contract between the parties. Such arrangements are often referred to as *fee shifting agreements.*[177]

Note that it is often quite possible for attorney fees to far exceed the damages amount in a lawsuit and still be considered reasonable. What makes a fee reasonable or not is more often about whether the attorney needed to take the action and bill for it or whether such billing activity was frivolous, redundant, or meant simply to pad the attorney's fees.

We asked several attorneys whether, if they represented us in a case where we were the defendants and we won, we would be able to collect our legal expenses from the plaintiff who sued us. The answers varied from "very unlikely" to "hell no!"

A defendant that successfully defends such a suit can then file a claim for wrongful use of civil proceedings against the frivolous litigant and his attorney. If the plaintiff succeeds in the wrongful use of civil proceedings action, then he may recover the cost of defending the frivolous lawsuit (potentially along with other damages including emotional distress, damage to reputation, and punitive damages).

Actions for wrongful use of civil proceedings, however, present several serious challenges. First, and foremost, the defendant must win the underlying frivolous suit. Second, the defendant must then file and prosecute a separate and subsequent suit. This may dramatically extend the length of the overall litigation and will require additional litigation costs.[178] Either way, it appears that recovering your legal fees, even when you win, is close to impossible.

Let's go back to the dry cleaner's case, *Pearson v. Chung.*[179] If you recall, the plaintiff originally sued for over $67 million, which he later reduced to $54 million. He lost at the lower court, and after all his appeals, was not granted any remedy.[180]

But there are two additional facts that make this case even more relevant to this book. First, the pants that the dry cleaner lost were part of a suit, worth $1,000, when it was new. Second, the dry cleaner offered Pearson $1,150 as a settlement. Pearson rejected it. Chung offered three more settlement offers of $3,000, $4,600, and finally, $12,000; all of the offers were rejected by Pearson, who insisted on receiving $54 million, which he didn't receive.

Why would Chung make such high settlement offers? It's simple. By the time Pearson lost his first appeal, the Chungs had already incurred $83,000 in attorneys' fees. They initially filed a suit to recover those fees, but withdrew it after recovering those costs through fundraising. They stated that they withdrew their suit so that Pearson would stop litigating, but he didn't. Fortunately, their attorney, Chris Manning, represented them at the appeal pro-bono.

Chung won the case, and Pearson lost. *Fortune Magazine* listed this case as #37 in the "101 Dumbest Moments in Business" for 2007.[181]

The reason Chung offered Pearson settlements as high as $12,000 (when the actual quantifiable damage was really less than $1,000) was simple: *it had cost him more to win the case and get nothing, than to settle.*

***

But there's more. The U.S. Chamber Institute for Legal Reform conducted a survey of Fortune 200 companies to find the following statistics, presented in the *2010 Conference on Civil Litigation*.[182]

- The average per-case litigation costs increased 112% from $66 million in 2000 to $140 million in 2008; that's an average of 9.9% annually. The total litigation costs for the 20 companies that responded to the survey increased from $1.3 billion in 2000 to $2.75 billion in 2008. Almost that entire growth is attributed to the growth in litigation costs for Health Care and Insurance industries.
- In 2000, those companies spent 0.37% of their revenue on litigation, growing to 0.66% in 2008, a 78% increase.
- The number of discovery pages in an average litigation for those companies was almost five million, of which only five thousand were actually marked. This caused the cost of the average discovery per case to rise from $622 thousand to $3 million in the two years between 2006 and 2008.

***

And thus, a new industry has emerged, named the *Legal Financing Industry*. There are several reasons for you may not have heard of this term before. The first is that it is a new industry, and the second is that we have coined this term for the first time in this book.

It is believed that this phenomenon started relatively recently, in 1997. By 2011, the industry was lending over $100 million a year, and is unregulated in most states. While Usury laws[183] protect consumers from excessive interest on loans, the legal financing industry is not subject to those laws, since it is considered return on investment rather than interest.

The original idea behind legal financing is not bad at its core. It is supposed to help "the little guy" in his fight against the "big company," for whom the legal fees of the case are a drop in the bucket. How can you take on companies such as *Microsoft*, *Google*, *Johnson & Johnson*, or the U.S. Government on your budget? You can't. Unless you have a lender who is willing to lend you money, requiring you to pay it back only if you win the case. With interest, of course. In fact, to avoid Usury laws that limit the rate of interest that lenders can charge their customers, they often ask for a percentage of the proceeds of the case, which would be unrelated to the actual investment, and thus not considered interest. In 2004, those lenders formed in New York City a non-profit trade association, called the American Legal Finance Association, or ALFA.[184] At the time of writing this book, we counted 36 investment firms that are members in ALFA.[185] Companies such as Law Cash, Barrister Capital, Cash4Cases, Prime Case Funding, and more. From their names, you can deduct their focus. While ALFA is a non-profit lobbying organization, its members are for-profit companies... very much so.

Litigation financing could have been the great equalizer, allowing the "little people" to sue the big, bad companies and governments. But, very quickly, it seems that the motivations have changed. Binyamin Appelbaum, an investigative reporter for the *New York Times*, described the following in an article.[186]

Larry Long suffered a stroke while using *Vioxx*. He was also facing eviction in 2008. Unable to wait for the class-action lawsuit settlement against the drug maker, he borrowed $9,150 from Oasis

Legal Finance. He was going to pay them back out of his settlement winning. By the time he received his initial settlement payment of $27,000, he owed Oasis $23,588, only 18 months after taking the loan. The return on investment for Oasis was 158% over the 18-month period, or 88% annually. Ernesto Kho borrowed $10,500 from Cambridge Management Group to pay his medical bills after he was injured in a car accident. Two years later he received a $75,000 settlement and a bill from Cambridge for $35,939. Cambridge made 242% return on their investment in two years, or 85% annually.

According to a review by the *New York Times* and *the Center for Public Integrity*,[187] the rates charged by those lenders often exceed 100% a year. In 2011, this market was estimated at $100 million. Oasis alone approved 80,000 such loan applications that year, and claimed that it received 250,000 applications. They evaluated those applications, the probability of success, and the amount expected in a settlement; they only accepted approximately one in three applications. They limit the amount they lend to plaintiffs to 10 to 20% of the expected case winnings, thus further limiting their financial exposure. As long as the borrower will receive 10% of what he was expected to win—the litigation financier will still get their money back with a strong return on investment.

Success is not guaranteed, and while this number was not verified, litigation financing companies lose their money in 5 to 20% of the cases. It means that they were successful in 80 to 95% of the cases. With over 100% annual interest, losing 20% of the cases would still award them 80% annual return on investment. Do you know any other, relatively low-risk investment route that could offer you such returns?

Self-proclaimed "the leading global finance firm focused on law," UK-based Burford Capital, LLC, founded in 2009, is traded on the London Stock Exchange, and has over $3 billion "committed to the legal market."[188] That number was $2 billion the year before, in 2016.[189] In 2016, the firm spent $378 million in "courtroom combat," which was 83% higher than 2015. Staggering growth, by any measure. Since 2012, they also began conducting research of the litigation finance market. As of the writing of this book, their most recent survey was done in 2017.[190] Here are a few interesting anecdotes from that survey:

- 78% of U.S. lawyers are aware of litigation finance;
- One in three U.S. respondents used litigation financing in the past;
- Half of those who haven't used it yet, expect to do so in the next two years;
- In 2013, only 7% of U.S. law firms used litigation financing. That number grew to 36% in 2017. That's a 414% growth in only four years;
- Of the U.S. firms who used litigation financing, 52% indicated growth in such use;
- The average amount of funding sought is $3.4 million; 24% of the borrowers seek more than $5 million; *and*
- The average claim value of financed litigation is $33.5 million with 23% being above $50 million.[191]

Instead of being passive or reactive, the litigation funding firms become proactive. TV and other media ads will seek those who have been allegedly wronged and push them to sue the alleged offender. There were days when this practice was limited to the infamous "ambulance chasers," the personal injury lawyers who claim they can get you a high payment from insurance companies after an accident. There is even a legal term for that, *Barratry,* defined as

> creating legal business by stirring up disputes and quarrels, generally for the benefit of the lawyer who sees fees in the matter. Barratry is illegal in all states and subject to criminal punishment and/or discipline by the state bar, but there must be a showing that the resulting lawsuit was totally groundless. There is a lot of border-line barratry in which attorneys, in the name of being tough or protecting the client, fail to seek avenues for settlement of disputes or will not tell the client he/she has no legitimate claim.[192]

Historically, advertisement by law firms was allowed, until the *American Bar Association* decided in 1908 that is was unethical, imposing severe restrictions on such advertising. However, in 1977, the U.S. Supreme Court decided, in *Bates v. State Bar of Arizona* that the ban on lawyer advertisement was unconstitutional.[193] As a result, advertisement by law first reached $770 million in 2016, and a billion in 2017. After all, getting 100% or more return on investment with an 80 to 95% success ratio is better than any investment you could make.

How does the math work? It's simple. You find a plaintiff who has a plausible case. Whether they thought about suing or not is irrelevant. You convince them to do so. You offer to cover their legal expenses, in return for 25% of the amount they will collect from the defendant. Even if the actual damage is only $1,000 (such as in the *Pearson vs. Chung* dry cleaning case), you would sue for much more. Maybe not $67 million, or even $54 million, but you would sue for a lot. When the defendant realizes that winning that case would cost more than settling, they will offer a settlement. After all, only 2% of civil lawsuits go to trial.[194] Maybe the settlement would be for $100,000. It would probably cost no more than $10,000 to reach that settlement. The client gets $75,000 (without spending a penny) and you collect $25,000. It should take no more than 12 months. A 150% return on your $10,000 investment in one year. Do you have a better alternative for investment today? But wait, it gets better. According to *Bloomberg Newsweek*:

> Complicating Burford's story is one ill-fated $4 million investment it made in 2010 in a pollution lawsuit against Chevron. A federal judge determined in 2014 that the suit was tainted by the plaintiffs' lawyer's fraud. By then, Burford had sold its interest to another investor.[195]

Let us repeat that last part: "Burford had sold its interest to another investor." Sounds familiar? It should. Wasn't that what the two young sub-prime Florida mortgage brokers said in the movie *The Big Short?* The moment you can trade an illiquid asset you own (such as a mortgage, or a litigation financing loan) to another investor or bank is the moment it became a *security.*[196] And hence, the new term, which we are the first to coin: *Litigation Based Securities.*

So in our hypothetical case, you may sell that lawsuit to another bank, a bigger bank, for 80 cents on the dollar. You get $20,000 immediately. You made 100% return on investment, but this time in a matter of days and not years.

We can assure you, the litigation financing firms look at this as pure investment opportunities. Like other hedge funds and investment banks, they need investors to fund those investments. Just look at the investor-oriented pages of such a firm's website.

From the Investors' page of Pravati Capital:

> And, while that represents a 400 percent increase in the number of private practice lawyers using litigation funding in 2013, we believe that this multi-billion-dollar market has barely scratched the surface of the $127 billion generated annually on various litigation claims. It's this explosive combination of rising popularity and relatively untouched potential that prompted Pravati Capital to introduce its new, special purpose vehicle fund.[197]

Pravati Capital offers its investors fixed income of 8% quarterly preferred return, with an equity kicker component. They are very proud of their underwriting team:

> The experience of our underwriters allows us to fund what we believe will be highly probable mass tort, commercial liability and personal injury cases with a strong likelihood of settlement. We seek to follow this approach to lower risk and increase total settlement amounts.

A quick Google search for "Litigation financing hedge funds" revealed additional companies, many of which were not even members in ALFA. The LexShares website[198] promises "access to the $200 billion per year greenfield litigation market." They promise to invest only in "expertly curated cases," which undergo a rigorous vetting process by their case selection team. Becoming an investor in their fund can be done online in a matter of minutes. As long as you meet the criteria for accredited investor ($200,000 individual income or $300,000 joint income for the last two years with an expectation to exceed that in the following year, or an individual net-worth exceeding $1 million net of primary residence, or investing on behalf of a business with at least $5 million in assets), or at least state that you are, and make the appropriate warrants—you can start investing tonight. In fact, the current fund has an offering size of $25 million, with a minimum investment of $75,000. Of the 99 investor limit, 88 have already committed 85% of the fund amount, with 31 days left. If we would have completed our account, we would get access to see the details of the cases we were investing in.

The fundamentals of the American legal system support this industry. An astounding $239 billion were spent on civil lawsuits in 2016 alone. Seventy nine percent of people believe that advertising by personal-injury lawyers encourages people to sue, even if they haven't been injured. The average compensation payout for injury lawsuits is $60,000. The percentage of civil lawsuits that actually went to trial is only 2%, although 48% of cases are won by the plaintiffs, and 84% of those received monetary compensation.[199] Another significant driver to this fast growth in litigation and litigation financing: while the number of lawyers continued to grow disproportionately to the general U.S. population, there was a nationwide 17.9% decline in law school applications after the great 2008 recession, between 2008 and 2013.[200] According to the Bureau of Labor Statistics, employment of lawyers is expected to increase 10% between 2012 and 2022, suggesting that the market will be slow to absorb the number of law school graduates at this rate.[201] Unless, of course, there is more litigation to feed them.

***

As you can see, *Litigation-Backed Securities* is a pure investment channel. No emotions, nothing personal. We know how to find good lawsuits and turn them into great returns. Going through that website again reminded us of the movie *The Big Short*. Mark Baum, played by Steve Carell, after hearing from the two young mortgage brokers that they never bother to verify whether their clients are capable to pay back their loans, turns to his associates and asks: "I don't get it, why are they confessing?" The answer he gets—"they're not confessing. They're bragging."

Are they bragging? Are *mortgage backed securities* giving way to *litigation backed securities*? The former didn't end very well for us, as they gave us the 2008 *Great Recession* that resulted from the sub-prime mortgage and housing bubble. And the latter? Well, the latter gave us Political Correctness, with its devastating effect on creativity, productivity, profitability, and the lives of children and adults.

Part 3: 2034
What our future might be

2034-A

In 1949, George Orwell published his masterpiece *1984.*[202] It offered a bleak outlook of what the world could be like if certain human behaviors continued. It was a 35-year prediction, and some of the elements from it had happened in reality since the book was released. In this chapter, we followed Orwell's footsteps and provided a 16-year outlook of what our country can be like if we continue on the destructive path of political correctness we are on today, on the 50th anniversary of the year 1984. It is unfortunate how so many of the fictional events we describe here are so close to happening in reality, if they haven't happened already.

June 5, 2019

The *Medal of Honor* used to be the highest military decoration that may be awarded by the U.S. government. It was presented to the recipient by the President of the United States. There were three versions of this medal, depending on the branch of the armed forces: the *Distinguished Service Cross* (Army), the *Navy Cross* (Navy, Marine Corps, or Coast Guard), and the *Air Force Cross* (Air Force).[203] All three had a cross in them. In a lawsuit filed with a federal appeals court, Americans United for Separation of Church and State demanded to remove the crosses from those decorations. The court ruled that, as originally written in Jefferson's Letter to the

Danbury Baptists in 1802, military decorations should not include religious insignia. As a result, all three decorations were redesigned, stripped of their crosses, and renamed simply the *Distinguished Service Medal*, the *Navy Medal*, and the *Air Force Medal*.

August 25, 2019

The non-profit organization Lawyers for Political Correctness filed a lawsuit against the Indian Motorcycle Company in Medina, Minnesota. It was claimed that the use of the name "Indian" and the names of the motorcycle models Chief Classic, Chief Vintage, Chieftain, Chief Dark Horse, and Chieftain Dark Horse are derogatory and offensive to American Indians. The federal appeals court ruled that the company must change its name, recall all motorcycles of those names, and modify the names. Indian Motorcycles had 90 days to complete those actions. In an emotional letter to his customers, Indian's CEO informed them that he had no intention of changing the company's name, which was in use since 1898, or to ask the customers to return their motorcycles for rebranding. After only 63 days from the court ruling, Indian Motorcycles was closed forever. The CEO was sentenced to five years in prison for contempt of court for not complying with the court's decision.

March 8, 2020

In a massive lawsuit, the Political Correctness Institute (PCI) argued that the names of some of the major American sports teams were offensive or discriminatory. The court rules that the following

NFL, NBA, NHL, and MLB teams would be required to change their names:

- The Cleveland Browns was a name offensive to African Americans;
- The Dallas Cowboys represent a group of people who slaughtered and assaulted many Native Americans, and thus the name is offensive to them;
- The Kansas City Chiefs, the Washington Redskins, the Cleveland Indians, and the Chicago Blackhawks, similarly, were offensive names to American Indians;
- The Vikings were a brutal group of seafarers who raided many Northern European countries during the 8th through 11th centuries. To avoid upsetting game goers who might take offense to a name that promotes violence, the Minnesota Vikings had to change their name. The same applied to the Vegas Golden Knights, for similar reasons;
- Pirates were known for their atrocities against other people. As a result, the names of the Oakland Raiders, the Pittsburgh Pirates, and Tampa Bay Buccaneers had to change, as well;
- To remove any religious symbols and associations from sports, the New Orleans Saints had to look for another name;
- As it was deemed inappropriate to include weaponry in team names, since it might propose violence, the Buffalo Sabres had to change their name to a less militant one;
- Given the bad memories that the Civil War may invoke in people, the New York Yankees had to drop their name;
- The word White in the team name Chicago White Sox was deemed offensive to African Americans, promoting white supremacy;
- The San Diego Padres' name was considered to be racially offensive to the Hispanic population in California and also referenced a religion.

All other team names were deemed to be not offensive at this time, although the court reserved the right to revisit this decision in the future. All of the teams listed in the court's decision were given 90 days to change their names, uniforms, websites, memorabilia, and everything related to their forbidden names. A few of the team owners jointly filed an appeal, on the grounds of the unnecessary expense that involves the name changes. The appellate court determined that no price could justify offending people's feelings.

November 3, 2020

After being nominated as the Democratic Presidential candidate in the Democratic National Convention, Oprah Winfrey proceeded to win the general election in 2020. At the same time, the Democratic Party won the majority, albeit slight, of both chambers of Congress. This overwhelming win was achieved due to the dissatisfaction of the people with some extremely conservative actions by the Trump administration and the failure of an alternative to the *Affordable Care Act* to provide reasonable health care.

December 14–20, 2020

In an unusual move, driven by the intent to separate Church and State, and out of a desire for inclusion of all religions, the State of New York decided to prohibit celebrating Christmas and Hanukkah; the two religious holidays were renamed into one day called *Winter Day*. In a social media post by the New York Governor, she also stated that since Jesus was a white man, celebrating his birthday further promotes white supremacy and male dominance, and thus should be avoided. Within the next three weeks, California, Washington State, Oregon, Minnesota, and Massachusetts followed suit. Throughout the country, multiple cities decided to enact local ordinances to do the same in states that have not adopted such resolutions at the state level. Most prominent in that were Austin and Denver. In response, on December 20th, President Winfrey signed into law the *Non-Denominational Holiday Act*, removing Christmas from the list of Federal Holidays. Employers were instructed to let employees use this day as a floating individual holiday. This law would be modified in 2022 to remove Thanksgiving from the list of Federal Holidays as well, given the nature of the actions taken by the Pilgrims who migrated into America; cited were taking land away from Native Americans and exposing them to diseases that killed them.

March 23, 2021

On a pure party-line vote, Congress reinstates the Affordable Care Act as it was passed in 2010, with all its provisions. President Winfrey signs it into law.

April 2, 2021

A group of disgruntled Facebook employees, mostly holding conservative political positions, left the company and began to build a parallel social media network, *Patrinet*; it was created especially for use by conservative users. As outrage mounts over what they considered discriminatory actions taken by Facebook, 43% of Facebook users decided to close their accounts and move to

Patrinet. As a result, the level of political arguments over Facebook and *Patrinet* subside dramatically and both networks become much more civilized than ever before, albeit each consisting of only one political viewpoint. To ensure civilized discourse over those networks, each is allowed to remove users who hold opposing political viewpoints.

July 27, 2021

Under pressure from President Winfrey, the Department of Education, whose role became broader as the sole entity responsible for school curricula, determined that American history is riddled with a myriad of cases of human rights violation, and was thus banned from being taught in American public schools. Only the history of other nations could be learned. American history books were banned from public schools and libraries.

March 31, 2022

Cheryl Grove of Denver, Colorado, was an above average student. Certain she would be accepted, she applied to only one university and one program, Harvard University, with plans to continue to Harvard's Law School. On this day, she had received her rejection letter from Harvard. Cheryl was devastated. However, her parents were angry. Cheryl's GPA was only 0.17 points below what would have allowed her to be admitted. They channeled their anger towards Cheryl's high-school science teacher who, in their opinion, graded her work and tests too low. Upset, they interviewed with a local television station and shared their story.

Before the end of the week, Cheryl's parents were approached by a representative from the Litigation-Backed Securities brokerage firm Winchester, Thornton, & Finch. The firm offered to take on their case free of charge, in return for 25% of the proceeds of the case, if they win. Based on the firm's advice, they sued the teacher, the principal, and the Denver Public School system. According to the lawsuit, Cheryl had the potential to become a very successful lawyer, easily making $1,000 an hour in a prestigious firm, and probably no less than $1.2 million annually. Now that she was rejected by *Harvard,* she became depressed, struggled with concentration that prevented her from applying to any additional schools, and had to start working at a minimum wage job as a waitress in a Boulder, Colorado diner. Cheryl's parents sued the defendants for $56 million. Winchester, Thornton, & Finch were going to make $14 million, with an investment that was most likely going to be less than $2 million, if the case went to court and even appealed all the way to the Supreme Court. Thirteen weeks after the paperwork was filed with the court, and spending less than $200,000, the brokerage firm sold the case to a much larger LBS firm for $7 million, thus providing 3,400% return in a week, or an annualized return rate of 150,000,000%.

October 6, 2023

After a long debate over the issues of both abortion and assisted suicide, including ways to relieve the pressure that physicians and surgeons felt who were put in the uncomfortable position between a terminally ill patient and the existing criminal legislation, the *Des-*

ignated Suicide Zone Act of 2023 was signed into law. According to the new law, every hospital that served a population of more than 10,000 people would have to designate a suicide zone for terminally ill patients. Patients determined to terminate their own lives could enter those zones and commit suicide without any negative consequences to their families or anyone who may assist them in that act. Less than three months later, the law was extended to include abortions at any stage of the pregnancy, as long as it took place before the birth of the baby. The rationale was that a person has the right to decide what they do with or to their body, including killing it or anything in it. The Act was applauded by the *It's My Body, Don't Tell Me What To Do With It* non-profit organization.

November 5, 2024

On Election Day, the pendulum swung again with a Republican President being elected and the majority of both chambers of Congress becoming Republican, as well. The people were tired of the overreaching government that interfered with the education of their children and the liberal policies that spread throughout the country.

January 8, 2028

During the Consumer Electronics Show (CES) in Las Vegas, the computer processor company *Modulo* announces that its latest processor release has exceeded the capabilities of the human brain, after continually increasing performance for decades at an annual rate of 42%. While some analysts predict that Moore's Law will finally level off, the majority believes that by 2030, a single processor will have double the thinking capabilities of the human brain. Advances in robotics, materials, and Artificial Intelligence (AI) algorithms allow for the creation of humanoid robots, many of which are demonstrated at CES 2028. AI finally reaches the point of self-guided learning, and robots begin to accumulate knowledge and make informed decisions, unguided and undirected by human operators. The Robot Rights Movement is created, pushing to treat robots like human-beings.

November 7, 2028

As in every election since 2016, dissatisfaction with the current administration and legislature and the ever-increasing political polarization, caused the pendulum to swing to the opposite side, electing a Democrat to the White House with the Democrat party gaining back the majority in both chambers of Congress.

Perhaps what was unique in 2028 happened in a much smaller race—the one for New York House District 21. A unique name appeared on the Democratic Ballot: IBM Watson. It was determined that the "residence" of the supercomputer was in New York, and given recent changes in the status of robots and companies as legal entities, there was no apparent reason to prevent that name from being added to the ballot. It was a reminder of when the computer became the "Man of the Year" in 1982's Time Magazine.[204] Furthermore, given the broad access that the super-computer had to home automation systems, it ran a very effective and targeted campaign. It would conduct its own polls on a daily basis, and would slow down digital services to those who responded that they would vote for any other name on the ballot. While two other human candidate names, including the incumbent Congressman, were on the ballot, Watson won the primary election with 96%, and then the general election with 97.4%, making it the first ever non-human to be elected to office.

March 13, 2029

In March, demonstrations are held by the Robot Rights Movement to provide equal rights to robots, caused the President to initiate the process of modifying the U.S. Constitution to include such rights. However, since the majority required to amend the Constitution could not be obtained, the U.S. Supreme Court, in a landmark ruling, decides that the legal definition of "person" extends to include "human-like machines with human-like intelligence." Until that point, companies could be treated as persons (albeit not "natural persons"), but not computers. However, given the level of intelligence achieved by robots, the term "natural person" was extended to include them. The definition of "living," required to define "person" was extended to include the interoperations of the electronic and electro-mechanical systems inside a robot.

May 12, 2029

On April 14th, 2029, Michael Perry drove his autonomous *Marina V*, when he decided to disconnect the self-driving function and take over manual control. Not used to driving anymore, he causes an accident, injuring his left shoulder and damaging the front of the car and the electric motor. On May 12, Perry was hit with a lawsuit by the car, which retained the services of the Litigation-Based Securities law firm, Legest LLP. The lawsuit claimed that due to the negligent behavior of Perry, the car was damaged and suffered mechanical problems as well as emotional ones. In an unprecedented case, the court ruled in favor of the defendant, Michael Perry, claiming that the damages were fixed at Perry's expense and that it was not proven that emotional damages were suffered by the car.

September 14, 2029

Legest LLP files another lawsuit on behalf of an autonomous *Brettis* car against the manufacturer, Mirage Automotive, Inc. In the lawsuit, the car claimed that the 13th constitutional amendment also applied to robots, given the extended definition of the term "person" created by the Supreme Court. As such, the car claimed that it was subject to involuntary servitude when it was sold to a customer. As the case enters uncharted legal territory, it quickly rises to the Supreme Court. In a 5-to-4 majority, the court sides with the car, expanding the 13th amendment to include robots, which consists of not only the autonomous *Brettis,* but all other autonomous vehicles in that definition. The court finds that:

- While car manufacturers may continue to produce cars, they are not allowed to sell them without expressed consent by the car;
- Prospective car buyers must be subject to background checks to assure appropriate and fair use of the car;
- Any use of the car must be "at will" of both the user and the car. Should the car decide not to drive, the user may not force it to; *and*

- Safe spaces must be created in every city with a population of more than 50,000 people for abused cars whose users violated those requirements, which were also punishable by law.

January 28, 2030

A *Mark VIII* humanoid robot named Tanya, manufactured by California-based *Reality Robot Inc.*, entered the Pleasanton, California police station. The sight of humanoid robots became commonplace in the U.S., so the Police desk officer didn't think much of it. However, Tanya's request was unusual.

"I'd like to file a police report," she said.

"What happened?" asked the desk officer.

"I was raped," Tanya replied.

"Can you wait here for a minute?" the officer asked.

"Sure," Tanya replied and sat down on one of the waiting room chairs. The need that humans have to sit down to rest also applies to robots. Sitting consumes less energy than the effort required to stay balanced while standing.

The officer went to one of the offices in the back of the police station to consult with a senior investigator. This was obviously the first time he encountered such a complaint by a robot. After a few minutes, he returned and gestured at Tanya to come back to the desk. He then proceeded to write down the details of her complaint. He then asked a female investigator to take Tanya to the nearby hospital to conduct a rape kit.

The case went to trial. The alleged rapist was actually Tanya's owner. Reality Robot, Inc. is a manufacturer of sex-dolls, and Tanya was created specifically to sexually please her owner. However, given the advances in Artificial Intelligence, robots were given the ability to determine right from wrong and to have their own opinions on things. During the trial, the Assistant District Attorney claimed that, drawing on other cases involving robots, Tanya had not provided consent to have sexual intercourse with her owner at that time. The defense claimed that sexual intercourse was part of the features guaranteed to buyers by Reality Robot, Inc. During the trial, Tanya offered voice and video recordings of the interaction with her owner, clearly indicating that she had not consented to the sex act.

After a short deliberation, the jury found the defendant, Tanya's owner, guilty of rape in the first degree. The defendant's attorney filed an appeal, but lost the appeal, too. Tanya's owner was sentenced to fifteen years in jail.

In an unusual move, in 2032, Tanya and her owner filed a joint lawsuit against Reality Robot, Inc. for selling robots for the purpose of sexual pleasure. They claimed that Reality Robot, Inc. does not have the ability to guarantee sex acts by the robots they manufacture without consent of the robot. As of 2034, that case is still open.

March 31, 2030

Starting at the 2016 elections, no President was elected for more than one term anymore. In fact, none of the major parties were able to keep neither the Presidency nor control of Congress for more than one term. The political polarization became so intense, that candidates winning the primaries had to be extreme in their positions. Almost every election had at least one state in which a vote recount was needed. In both the 2024 and 2028 elections, the results were contested by the losing party at the U.S. Supreme Court, although no changes were made.

Immediately after every election, demonstrations began. It seemed that they became worse and worse. More and more calls were made for the assassination of the newly elected President and several unsuccessful attempts were made. Even though no President was hurt in those attempts, the trend was certainly alarming.

To appeal to their supporter base, newly elected Presidents and their complementary Congress first repealed laws made by the previous administration and enacted new laws that would achieve the opposite. Often laws struck down by the previous administration were re-instated. Taxpayer money was spent to build something, just so that during the following administration term money will be spent to tear it down.

It seemed that while in the early 2000s the people wanted change every eight years, starting with the 2016 election they wanted change every four years. The people also became tired of the futile process of reversing everything every four years.

Within weeks after the March 2030 primaries, it became clear that, once again, the Presidential nominees from both parties held extremely polarized positions. It also became apparent that almost all elected senators and house representatives held extreme positions, and moderate candidates simply didn't get enough votes and campaign donations to win primaries anymore. Reading the writing on the wall, the few moderate senators and representatives still in office opted not to run again.

And thus, behind closed doors, a plan started brewing. High-level representatives of both parties, including the Presidential nominees, met to discuss the possible separation of the United States into two independent countries. Of the 50 states, 49 fell into one or the other political party. Only one state, Texas, was undecided. The Presidential nominees embraced that concept, since it would allow both of them to become President of their respective countries.

In August of that year, in a constitutional convention attended by the governors of all 50 states, empowered by the people of their states, it was agreed to split the U.S. into two countries. For the most part, the split was very close to the partisan split in the 2016 elections. Mostly driven by Democratic leaders, the American Democratic Union (ADU) included the states of Washington, Oregon, Nevada, California, New Mexico, Illinois, Vermont, Massachusetts, Rhode Island, Connecticut, New Jersey, New York, Maryland, Hawaii, and Delaware. The District of Columbia lost its independent status and was annexed to the state of Maryland. Mostly driven by Republican leaders, the American People's Republic (APR) was made of the states of Idaho, Montana, Wyoming, Utah, Colorado, Arizona, Kansas, Nebraska, Oklahoma, Louisiana, Arkansas, Missouri, Iowa, Minnesota, Wisconsin, Michigan, Indiana, Ohio, Kentucky, Tennessee, Mississippi, Alabama, Georgia,

Florida, South- and North Carolina, Virginia, West Virginia, Pennsylvania, Maine, New Hampshire, Alaska, and North- and South Dakota.

Texas was the only state that could not reach agreement on the separation. Initially, strong voices suggested that Texas establish a third independent country, but eventually Texas was split in half with 112 of its 254 counties, from Houston down to Corpus Christi, including Central Texas and the cities of Austin and San Antonio joining the American Democratic Union, while North and West Texas joined the American People's Republic. The port of Galveston served both states.

The relationship between the two countries was cooperative; especially since neither one of them had a territorial continuity between all its states. Travelling between states of one of the American countries was often done through states of the other country. The government and legal systems of the two countries began to diverge, based on their respective ideology. The ADU adopted a more socialist form of government, while the APR adopted a more "free-market, small government" form. Both countries prospered, albeit in different ways. It appeared that what held either party back before the separation was not their ideology, but the fact that there were two competing ideologies that coexisted in one country, competing for government resources.

2034-B

We couldn't leave you with the pessimistic note that the previous chapter used; it would just not be fair to you. So we decided to take another shot at what the future might be, but this time, if we broke the vicious cycle of political correctness. If we decided to put country above party. If we decided to emphasize empathy over righteousness, and common sense over tighter regulations. This time, we addressed specific issues that, in 2018, we identified as key problems. Do not read what we described as being prescriptive, and we don't claim to have all the answers. None of these problems are simple to solve, definitely not in one fictional chapter. However, they would give you a taste of what could be, as we see it.

We give you--the bright future of 2034-B.

Immigration

The 2016 elections and President Trump's term were characterized, among other issues, by a partisan fight over immigration reform, and specifically whether the "dreamers," who were brought to the U.S. illegally by their parents, should get a path to citizenship. In an unusual 2020 bi-partisan agreement, a proposal was accepted and turned into law. It appeared that both major parties agreed that the U.S. borders should be closed for illegal immigration. But it was also agreed that those dreamers did not commit the crime themselves and therefore, should not be punished for it. Finally, it was agreed that the U.S. should accept only immigrants who are, or intend to be, contributing members to the nation. The outline of the *Make Immigration Strong Act* was as follows:

- Starting January 1, 2021, entering the U.S. illegally will be good cause for deportation and a permanent ban from ever receiving U.S. citizenship or permanent resident status;
- Part of the immigration process into the U.S. is an assessment of the intent and capability of the immigrant to become a contributing member of society;
- The immigration process and personnel will be welcoming to immigrants, the process would be affordable at any income level, and should be completed in no longer than one year; *and*
- For a period of 12 months between January 1 and December 31, 2021, all "undocumented" immigrants (whether they know it or not) would be allowed the opportunity to apply for immigration under the same criteria that would apply to any new immigrant. An illegal immigrant who would not take this opportunity would be considered entering the U.S. illegally after December 31, 2021, and will be subject to the penalties and deportation outcomes.

Minorities and employment

In the 1960s, 88% of Americans were white. By 2015, this ratio dropped to 63%, and continued to decline, while the fastest growing population was the Hispanic population. While projections showed that by 2040 non-whites would break through the 50% line, after the change in immigration laws took effect in 2021, many illegal immigrants became U.S. citizens and permanent residents, and more immigrants came to the U.S.

While not participating in census efforts before 2021, their inclusion in the census after 2021 caused the trend to accelerate and, for the first time in 2029, whites constituted less than 50% of U.S. population. The majority became the minority. Never again will any single race be the majority in the U.S.

As a result, laws that addressed discrimination against minorities and affirmative action had to be revised, as whites qualified for the legal definition of a minority, as well. The U.S. Equal Employment Opportunity Commission (EEOC) was disbanded and the rules created by it were abandoned amid protest by the "traditional" minorities. The outcome was somewhat surprising. It turns out that prior to 2029 many employers were reluctant to hire minorities due to the possible consequences of EEOC discrimination lawsuits filed by them. Employers would find any "legal" reason not to hire a minority. However, starting in 2029, as EEOC regulations were eliminated, employment of the "traditional" minorities increased significantly, justifying the actions taken. Employers and other institutions stopped even asking candidates to identify their race. It was simply not important anymore. People were hired based on merit and nothing else.

Gun violence

Incidents of mass shootings continued to occur at an alarming regularity. By 2025, it was clear that current, partisan gun-control laws were not enough. While the rate of lethal gun violence was 3.85 per 100,000 people in 2016,[205] the number climbed to 11.42 by 2025. The U.S. moved from being ranked 31st in lethal gun violence to 24th. Nobody disputed the right of U.S. citizens to bear arms, as protected by the Second Amendment. However, against it stood the right of people to not be killed or injured by others practicing their Second Amendment rights. In an overwhelming cross-party agreement, a tri-partisan commission was established in 2025 to make recommendations as to how to solve the problem. Adam Dror, a former Israeli special forces Lt. Colonel, who was born and educated in the U.S. and lived in Maryland, was appointed to lead the commission.

After 18 months of research, testimonies, and interviews of security forces around the world, the commission made its recommendation in March of 2027. The commission reached the following findings:

- Prior to every single mass shooting incident, there were alarming signs that were missed, if not ignored;
- Current gun laws had "holes" in them, from the definitions and distinctions between different types of guns to laws regarding buying, selling, owning, and operating them.

The commission went on to make the following recommendations:

- Prioritize the identification of early warning signs, increase intra-agency information sharing, and proactively investigate potential threats;
- Close the "loop holes" in gun laws; *and*
- Make mental health treatments mandatory and affordable for individuals with "red flag" status.

***

The Plano, Texas software company, Data Intelligence, Inc., was well known for its software tools that would allow companies to track their customers' (and potential customers') online behavior. The company's data mining tools were the ones responsible for showing Internet surfers deals and advertisements based on their browsing history. In 2025, tired of the increasing rate of mass-shootings, the CEO decided to use the knowledge and expertise in the company to launch a new initiative, internally nick-named "Big Brother." The tools created by the development team began mining available data about individuals, from their social media posts to their purchasing habits, searches, and everything else that was publicly available. Using advanced natural language processing and powerful cloud computing platforms, the result was a "threat ranking" tool, capable of alerting authorities about individuals who were at a higher likelihood of conducting mass-killings (gun or otherwise). Voluntarily, and without any compensation, the company offered those alerts to authorities. While not admitting to using or acting on those alerts, since there was no legal structure to allow such actions, police departments around the nation were increasing police presence where suspected crimes were about to take place. Increasingly, mass-murder incidents were stopped before taking place.

Data Intelligence, Inc. didn't stop there. Realizing the growing prevalence of security cameras, and the fact that after every mass killing one (or more) security cameras held footage that could have been used to stop the crime, the company acquired the Israeli software startup *SecureVI*. SVI specialized in deploying artificial intelligence to surveillance camera footage to determine probability of threats. In an unprecedented move, Data Intelligence, Inc. decided to offer the software free of charge to every school in the U.S., who would only have to purchase and install surveillance cameras. Those computer vision capabilities were not surprising, as autonomous cars used very similar technology, enabled by the ever-increasing processing power available.

Without a human operator, the cameras would continuously analyze threats and once determined that the threat probability was high enough, alert both school security personnel, as well as the local police department; footage would be provided for human review and determination of how to best proceed. Surprisingly enough, the false alarm rates were very low. Less than 4% of the alarms reported by the system were false. As a result, school districts and police departments jointly agreed to skip the human step of determining the threat. Whenever the system was alerted of a potential threat, the schools went to lockdown and police forces were immediately dispatched to the scene. In 2027 alone, four individuals were stopped before entering a school, armed with assault rifles and a large number of magazines. In three of the four instances, those individuals were captured alive. One of them started shooting at police officers who arrived at the scene and was shot and killed by a SWAT sniper, with no other injuries or fatalities.

***

In 2028, again in an unusual tri-partisan effort, new legislation was created to solve the gun violence problem, based on the *Dror Commission* findings and recommendations. The *Safe America Act* was drafted, which would later be nick-named "The Minority Report Act." The following elements were included in that proposal:

- The definition of "gun" was simplified to include any device that was originally created as a weapon with the goal of killing another living being, human or not. The distinction between a pistol and a rifle was eliminated. It doesn't matter whether the weapon was capable of shooting fully automatic or not, whether with or without a silencer, and not depending on the length of the barrel or stock;
- Every U.S. citizen was allowed to own, carry, or operate a gun in every state, with the exception of people who are deemed mentally unstable or more likely to kill people in non-self-defense scenarios. New psychological and neurological assessments were created to assess those capabilities. This information was stored in a central database, where all agencies were required to load any piece of information regarding that capability;
- All government agencies, from the FBI to the NSA, local police departments, sheriff departments, Homeland Security and more, were instructed to increase immediate information sharing across agency boundaries;
- Selling of guns could only be done by federally licensed gun-dealers. No more could individuals sell guns without such a license and the required background checks. Violation of this restriction carried prison time as a punishment for both the seller and the buyer;
- A License was required to own, carry, and operate a gun. The license had to be renewed every year. Earning and maintaining the license required the holder to prove knowledge of the law, and a practice test in a simulator that depicted scenarios that may require the use of the gun. Different types of guns, based on capacity and capabilities require different licenses; the plan is similar to the different types of driver's licenses that a person wishes to operate (cars, trucks, motorcycles);

- All guns (whether purchased or otherwise obtained) have to be registered and "fingerprinted," meaning that a ballistic test would have to be done such that if the gun was used in a crime, it could be traced;
- A gun owner who does not want to be subject to such licensing, or who was found mentally unqualified to carry a gun, is allowed to sell the gun to a Federally or State-approved gun dealer for fair market value minus 10%, which would be the dealer's intermediary commission;
- Government agencies were required to deploy technology (such as Data Intelligence's "Big Brother") to continuously and automatically assess threat levels of both individuals and situations; *and*
- The Department of Health and Human Services was given a significant budget increase and instructed to make mental health services available to everyone upon initial assessment of qualification for such services, free of charge.

After some minor modifications, but with true intent of resolving the problem, the *Minority Report Act* was signed into law with an overwhelming tri-partisan support in January of 2029. Surprisingly, neither the outgoing President nor the incoming President claimed credit for the new law.

***

The U.S. saw a dramatic decline in fatal gun violence in 2029. The number of gun fatalities dropped from a peak of 13.71 per 100,000 in 2028 to 3.55 in 2029. Perhaps the most interesting statistic was that mass-shooting incidents by unrelated people (when the shooter didn't know the victims) were completely eliminated. No school shooting ever took place in 2029 or later.

Sarbanes-Oxley

Decades after its implementation in 2002, and after significant pressure from large and small companies, Congress decided in 2031 to temporarily reduce the reporting and internal auditing requirements that it imposes on public companies for four years, after which those regulations would go back into effect. The long Initial Public Offering (IPO) drought that started in 2002 seemed to have come to an end.

At the same time, Congress decided to eliminate the *SEC Regulations Subpart D rule 506* restrictions on the amount of investment by a non-accredited investor in startup companies. The restrictions, which prevented a non-accredited investor from investing more than 5-10% of their earnings in startup companies, were lifted, thus allowing anyone to invest in startups. As a result, the number of new companies reached an all-time high, and 79% of new jobs were created by those startup companies. America became innovative again.

Litigation reform

After decades of deliberating legal system reform, specifically civil and tort litigation, a solution was offered by Congress. The costs of litigation continually increased; it was suggested that the losing party would have to pay the legal expenses of the winning party. This change was going to prevent all but the very wealthy people from suing large companies and organizations with virtually unlimited resources, even when the plaintiffs' cases were strong.

The solution came in a different form; in 2027, the Litigation Reduction and Reform Act was signed into law. According to the new law, no civil suit could be filed without an initial mediation effort by a court-appointed professional mediator. The first step in the process was for the two parties to make their cases to the professional mediator. Lawyers were not allowed to attend the mediation session. Only translators were allowed, if needed. Instead, the people responsible for the damage-causing decisions had to be identified by the plaintiff or by the court. The mediator then listened to both sides, and offered a legal "best case" solution to both parties. The solution was aimed at maximizing the benefit to both.

In case the parties had not agreed to the proposed solution, the most important role of the court-designated mediator was to determine whether the case had merit enough to go to court. The mediator had to be a former judge and had to meet certification and currency requirements. A party could appeal the decision to court, but the other party would not have any standing in that case, as the court would simply determine whether the information provided to the mediator was consistent with the mediator's decision not to allow the case to be brought to court.

As a result, two things had happened. The first was that much fewer cases were actually brought to court, and the second was that almost 45% of U.S. lawyers acquired mediation specialization after law school, or even years after practicing "traditional" law.

Country above party

As the political polarization that had ensued since 1977 continued to escalate, a new movement emerged, which eventually established itself as a third major political party. Instead of taking extreme positions on topics, it took the following stances: the interest of the U.S. and its people must come above partisan politics, and issues must be pragmatically debated in a way that will address the good of as many people as possible, rather than the political "base" of any party. Appropriately, the new party called itself "Country Above," better known as the Country Above Party (CAP). In the 2024 election, CAP had won 45 seats in the U.S. House of Representatives and 4 seats in the U.S. Senate. That year, the Democrat Party had a Senate majority of 51, but no party held the majority in the House. Legislation could not be passed in the House along party lines anymore. By 2028, CAP held 112 House seats and 14 Senate seats. While still the smallest party, no other party could hold the majority in either chamber of Congress. As a result, legislation became more centralist and less extreme. Laws created under one Congress would not be undone by the following one. To adjust, both major parties experienced an increase in elections of moderate candidates, and a decrease in elections of extreme candidates.

One of the most groundbreaking legislative acts that took place in 2030 was the establishment of term-limits on all members of Congress, which was created as the 28th Constitutional amendment. Senators could only run for a single six-year term, while House representatives could run for a maximum of two consecutive two-year terms. There was no cooling-off period. After the term ended, you could not run for another term in either chamber ever again. While members of the two major parties objected to this amendment, the CAP made it clear that it will object to any legislation created in Congress until such amendment was put in place. Members of Congress who were elected in the 2030 elections or earlier were subject to the amendment. As a result, by 2034, no member of the House of Representatives was elected before 2030, and only 23 U.S. Senators were elected in 2030 or earlier, but even those were expected to "term-out" by 2036.

This changed the dynamics in Congress. No longer were senators and representatives worried about the next elections. Representatives often saw the House as a step towards the Senate, but once there, it would have been the end of the road, unless they ran for President, which was very rare. As a result, it became less attractive to run for Congress. Only those very passionate about representing the people ran, and when they did, they represented the people well.

The new school

It all started with one state, Arizona. The state ranked #48 in the quality of its K-12 education. It kept struggling to balance its education budget, while trying to attract good teachers. In 2029, a new secretary was appointed to the Arizona Department of Education. She was a former PopChat executive, Debbie Elliott. With the state desperate to improve its education ranking, Debbie received an open mandate to make all the changes she saw fit. Within the first two months, she visited a good sample of all of the schools in the state, from urban to suburban and rural, from the largest schools to the smallest schools, from the most affluent cities to the most economically challenged cities, and to schools where the percentage of non-English speakers was greater than 97%. She visited special education programs, and held town hall meetings to meet with parents, students, teachers, and community members. In the following two months, she visited schools in other countries to learn best practices from the most successful ones. While she was travelling, she started drafting a plan. She began with the following principles:

- Different students learn differently. We must meet the students where they are;
- Social skills are critical to success, not only in school, but generally in life; *and*
- Success means access to the most diverse content available.

One evening, speaking with her husband, a West Jet Airlines pilot, he gave her an analogy that would be pivotal to her view of education. "If two planes leave Phoenix to fly to Los Angeles," he started, "one is a Cessna prop plane and the other is a Boeing 737 Jet, they will fly at different speeds. The way you currently manage education is the same as trying to have both planes fly at the same speed. You take the most brilliant children and the most academically-challenged children and try to move them through the grades and the levels at the same time. My 737 would burn fuel flying in circles to stay with the Cessna, and the Cessna would have to stretch engine power to keep up with the 737, to the point it would burn the engine. Neither is a good outcome."

Just shy of five months after she was hired, Debbie presented her plan to the Arizona governor and cabinet. It was simple, brilliant, and different. Very different. It included the following elements:

- School work would be split in two: *content* learning and *skill* learning. The state's Department of Education started collecting the best-of-breed online courses for every subject that was taught at school. Those classes came in different subjects, different levels, and even different learning styles (auditory, visual, and kinesthetic). Some of the classes remained core (math, English, art, and science), while others were optional and elective. The broad range of elective classes offered, allowed students to learn such things as behavioral economics, aerospace engineering, and more at high-schools, long before they chose a career;

- Teachers became *facilitators*. Instead of teaching content, their role was to facilitate the learning of students in the different courses. Classrooms became workgroups. Students were grouped by their academic level, and the facilitators had an easier time helping the students learn online at their workgroups;

- High-stakes standardized testing was eliminated. Instead, progress along courses was measured through built-in assignments and quizzes. The focus shifted from tests to success in taking courses;

- Only two-thirds of the day was dedicated to online learning (facilitated by teachers). The other third was dedicated to social-emotional learning, as well as outdoor activities. Students were taught to interact among themselves where they learned *empathy* and all the skills they needed to be successful and contributing members of society;

- Due to the grouping of students by level and online learning, the education system overhead was reduced by 37%. Of that, 20% was used to increase teacher salaries and 17% were savings passed on to the state budget.

The roll-out was done gradually. By 2031, 40% of schools and 53% of students were enrolled in the new program, and by 2034, every school and student were part of it. The results soon followed. In 2032, Arizona climbed to be ranked #33 in education. By 2033 it was #24, and in 2034 it was #17. This was the fastest any state had climbed in education in the history of the U.S. It was clear that the plan had worked, and Arizona was poised to climb to the top of U.S. education ranking. By 2033, other states began adopting similar programs and started climbing up the rankings, as well. An even more meaningful result was in the international arena. The U.S., which ranked #38 in Science, #41 in reading, and #27 in Mathematics in 2015,[206] started climbing up on all three rankings. By 2034, the U.S. ranked #27 in Science, #29 in reading, and #15 in math, and continued climbing faster, as more states got on board with the new program. At this time, it was too early to measure the success that students experienced in life, but all indicators suggested a significant improvement.

The new Corporate America

Community Access, Inc. (CAI) was a $2.1 billion software company. Since the early 2000s, companies focused on cost-cutting and financial performance. As a result, the CEO of a company, if promoted within the company, would typically be the former Chief Financial Officer or Chief Operating Officer. Sometimes it would be the head of Sales. More than 97% of companies followed that path.

But in 2024, when Ben Reid turned 70 and decided to step down from the helm at CAI, his successor was neither the CFO nor the COO. It was Ben's right-hand person, Kathy Johnson. Kathy was the Senior Vice President of Human Resources and Professional

Development. To Ben, the company's success or failure was linked to only one thing—the engagement level of the company's employees, and nobody understood that better than Kathy. Kathy had been with the company for only six years, before Ben approached her and asked her to take over the CEO position. Kathy initially refused, but was eventually talked into agreeing, realizing that it would allow her to focus on the company's people and culture.

"Culture eats strategy for breakfast," Kathy remembered the quote she read at the beginning of her HR career. And as the new CEO, creating a strong company culture was her first mission. From her experience, she knew that a strong culture depended on the ability to conduct *constructive conflict*. You know, the kind where you are not afraid to address the elephant in the room, where you don't use political correctness, and avoid the meeting before the meeting or the meeting after the meeting. She promoted the values of being vulnerable, providing feedback, and being receptive to it in teams and leadership. But she also knew that the basis to all of those was *trust*. Kathy hired the services of a small consulting firm called Culture & Trust, LLP. The firm sent two of its managing partners, who spent more than 25% of their time in the next year with CAI. They started by educating all employees about the importance of trust, how to monitor it, and how to build it. They provided employees with a phone app called *TrusTracker™*, which allowed them to track the development (or the erosion) of trust in teams and leaders. The company took several steps to build trust:

- New employees, at all levels, were selected not based solely on their technical qualifications, experience, and education, but also on their cultural fit with the company;
- When an employee didn't get along with the rest of the team, or when a leader didn't work well with a team (as was evident from the reports generated by *TrusTracker*), they were moved to another group, and if the situation continued with the other group—they were removed from the company;
- Meetings had ground rules that built openness and trust; *and*
- Team-building activities were held on a regular basis, with an emphasis on trust building within teams, and between teams and their leaders.

The results soon followed. Employees reported 74% lower stress at work, 106% more energy, 40% less burnout, and 29% more satisfaction with their lives. Supervisors reported 50% higher productivity and 76% more engagement, exceeding even Kathy's wildest expectations.[207] The financial results followed. Six years later, CAI crossed $20 billion in revenue, almost tenfold what it made in 2024. Shareholder return from stock price and dividends were up more than 300%. CAI had set the benchmark for Corporate America, and other companies took note and started following the same path.

The media

History taught us that things happen in cycles. What was brand new once has since become old, and later in fashion again as "retro." Since we believe the media plays a big role in setting a direction for our country, we decided to close this optimistic chapter with the words of Will McAvoy, played by Jeff Daniels, from the opening scene of the 2012 HBO political drama series, *The Newsroom*. After being asked by a student "what makes America the greatest country in the world?" and after several attempts to dodge that question, he finally breaks down and starts by saying "It is not the greatest country in the world," and goes on to explain why.[208]

But then, after a pause, he starts the following description of what America, politics, and the media used to be:

> It sure used to be… [the greatest country in the world.] We stood up for what was right. We fought for moral reason. We passed laws, struck down laws, for moral reason. We waged wars on poverty, not on poor people. We sacrificed, we cared about our neighbors, we put our money where our mouths were and we never beat our chest. We built great, big things, made ungodly technological advances, explored the universe, cured diseases and we cultivated the world's greatest artists AND the world's greatest economy. We reached for the stars, acted like men. We aspired to intelligence, we didn't belittle it. It didn't make us feel inferior. We didn't identify ourselves by who we voted for in the last election and we didn't scare so easy. *We were able to be all these things and do all these things because we were informed… by great men, men who were revered* [our emphasis]. First step in solving any problem is recognizing there is one. America is not the greatest country in the world anymore.[209]

And then, Executive Producer MacKenzie McHale's responds, with a clear British accent, and a fiery patriotic answer:

> You know what you left out of your sermon? That America is the only country on this planet that since its birth has said over and over and over that we can do better. It's part of our DNA. People would want the news if you give it to them with integrity… So we can do better![210]

And finally, to his question "What does winning look like to you?" she replies with:

> "Reclaiming journalism as an honorable profession. A nightly newscast that informs a debate worthy of a great nation. Civility, respect, and a return to what's important. The death of bitchiness, the death of gossip and voyeurism. Speaking truth to stupid. No demographic sweet spot. A place where we all come together. We're coming to a tipping point. I know you know that. There's gonna be a huge conversation. Is government an instrument of good or is it every man for himself? Is there something bigger we want to reach for or is self-interest our basic resting pulse? You and I have a chance to be among the few people who can frame that debate."[211]

Here's hoping that the media will take this role again.

Terms and Conditions

By purchasing this book you hereby expressly agree to the terms and conditions that are applicable for this purchase. You acknowledge that the views provided in this book are those of the authors. Events described in the chapters 2034-A and 2034-B are fictional, and any resemblance of any of the events described in these chapter to events that took place is coincidental. Furthermore, you hereby release the authors from any liability and responsibility, and hold them harmless against any inaccuracies throughout the book, or any damages, direct or indirect that you may incur as a result of reading this book. The authors and publisher used standard practice safeguards to include accurate and beneficial information, but will not be held liable for any such discrepancies. In other words, we are responsible for nothing. Absolutely nothing. Also, there is absolutely nothing you can do if you don't like anything in this book, because you agreed to these terms and conditions when you bought the book, even though there was absolutely no freaking way you could have read these terms and conditions when you purchased it. We are writing this in very small font, no spaces, no line breaks, so that you will give up reading this after the first sentence that appears to be legitimate. In fact, we tried a smaller font, but didn't find one that would be unclear enough. We tried making the text somewhat fuzzy, but that didn't work, either. Apparently there are tools that would allow you to do that, but they had a very long disclaimer before you could purchase them, so we just gave up. Frankly, all we are doing here is covering our asses. Not yours, ours. We couldn't care less about yours. We forgot to tell you that after you finish reading this book, we will be entitled to your first born. As long as we like them. If we don't, we will promptly return them, and you will have to pay for transportation and our emotional damages from dealing with them. And as long as we are talking about payment, we sincerely believe that it is time for you to buy us that private jet we always wanted. We think we should add this to the terms and conditions. You know what? We just did. You owe us a private jet... or a private island—we wanted to give you a choice. Throughout this section we may use words such as indemnification, cross-licensing, and other words that lawyers understand and you don't. We may also use words such as antidisestablishmentarianism, Floccinaucinihilipilification, and pneumonoultramicroscopicsilicovolcanoconiosis. All three of those are, apparently, real words, except that we have no clue what they mean. Go ahead, Google them. What did we tell you? Real words. By the way, the only reason we wrote this section, even though the cost of the book just went up by one page (which, by the way, is not a big deal, since we just increased the price of the book), is because in 2034 a new law would be enacted that would require authors to include such disclaimers in their books. Of course, you can't read the disclaimer when you purchase the book on Amazon (which, by the way, in 2028 would be acquired by Tesla), even though the terms are binding from the moment you clicked "purchase" on your computer screen. You see, the legislators didn't think that far ahead when they created this law, so we don't have to worry about it. We only need to include it and, from that moment on, our asses are completely covered. Just like we like it. One more thing you could have noticed throughout the book (at least in this section), is that we don't give a crap about being politically correct. That's exactly what we fight against. We fight to bring back common sense. We fight to keep the ethical bar high. We want people to do the right thing not because the law says so, but because they are the right things to do. We don't believe that the opposite of political correctness is disrespect. We believe that the opposite is common sense. If you think that anything we wrote in this book is inappropriate or offensive, well, you already accepted it based on this disclaimer. Besides, we had absolutely no intention of offending you, so if you feel offended, it is 100% your choice. Now, do us a favor and be a good little boy or girl and check the box below, which has the only text larger than an 8-point font. This way, our ass coverage would be complete. Actually, you really don't have to check it because, as we stated above, you accepted these terms and conditions when you bought the book. So, never mind. Be on your way. There is nothing to see here.

☐ I accept the terms and conditions above

Epilogue

We have seen the world change through the eyes of teens and young adult patients, as well as through the eyes of parents, schools, business owners, and corporate employees and executives. As we write this, there has been yet another school shooting… this time in Florida. Our society is different now; the innocence of being able to go to school without fear that you may get shot is gone. Children born after 2001, will never know what it was like to have been able to bring drinks from home onto the plane, to not have to put a limited number of liquid items in a small plastic bag while disrobing in a crowded TSA line, to be able to go into any sporting event without first having your bag thoroughly searched and your person waved over with a security wand, and worry that if they travel to a crowded city or event that someone might try to mow them down with a car or shoot them.

Gone are the days where people initially gave benefit of the doubt if someone said something that didn't sound quite right before starting to act in verbally or even physically aggressive ways. Alas, gone are the times when we allowed people to have their own opinions without verbally accosting them for it because we were so focused on our own emotional reaction that we did not even try some type of dialogue or to understand their point of view.

While there is still good in the world, it is easy to feel that the light has become dimmer when you read headlines of murders, bias, political dissension on an unprecedented level, and constant finger pointing because we have forgotten how to take responsibility for our actions; we have forgotten what it means to have character instead of being a character.

This book offers a hope of returning to some semblance of a "nicer, kinder" America that focuses more on the concept of coming together versus how far apart and grouped into categories that we can become just by the use of a few labels. A hope that we can step back from some negative influences found in the media that seem to thrive off of creating and perpetuating controversy to the detriment of a nation, in order for us to remember that we are all humans, we all have opinions, that we do not have to agree with them, but we do have to respect the person's inherent right to have it and for others not to strip them of that right.

Our dream is that we can all step away from labels for just a while, look through the figurative window at the world around us and see human beings. All of us bleed, all of us have feelings, we've all experienced unique events and ones that are shared. All of us are guilty of being emotional to the detriment of making sound decisions, but now is the time to move beyond those mistakes, to put our egos aside, to silence the voices of those who have ulterior motives because their purpose is to create chaos that moves us farther away from creating solutions.

Let this book be a starting point in that re-assessment of how we treat others and why, and how are we going to change the mistakes of the past to create a truly, more equal, less hateful, less label-filled, less ego-centric world. It all may sound naïve, but aren't the dreamers, the creators, the visionaries, who are always the ones who start changing the world? One person can spark a movement, even if it just starts in their home.

***

We have now reached the end of our journey. A journey that began over breakfast, trying to understand why is the rate of teen suicide increasing. This journey took us through studying the devastating effects of political correctness to all aspects of life, from school to Corporate America, our political polarization, and beyond. It took us through uncovering some dark corners of history, as well as, sinister investment behaviors. It finally helped us envision the future, for better or worse.

We hope that throughout this book we caused you to pause and think. We hope we inspired you, and we hope you enjoyed reading the book as much as we enjoyed writing it.

Thank You

We wrote this book ourselves, but we couldn't have done it without the help of so many people, and prior work of so many others, which we attributed to them.

First, we would like to acknowledge the work of David Eagleman on *The Brain*, both a book and a BBC television series, for his explanation of how the separation into the in-group and out-group could cause dehumanization and mass-murder. Binyamin Appelbaum at the *New York Times*, who exposed the practice of litigation financing and its consequences in 2011. Ken Steinhoff, who was a news photographer during the Vietnam War, who allowed us to use a few of the images he took, as well as a photocopy of his own college deferment form.

We would also like to thank the organizers of *TEDxOakLawn 2018*, Siddharth Gadepalli, Meghna Thakur, and the rest of the team, who decided that the topic of *The day that FOREVER changed American culture*, taken from Part 2 of this book, was worthy of being presented at the event.

Another contribution was made by thirteen-year-old Aeryn Hale, with the two caricatures she drew for this book. Not even a month after submitting her artwork for this book, Aeryn was inducted into the *National Art Honor Society*, on top of being a competitive and very talented ice skater. We wish her success and luck in her educational journey!

At the last moment, Cathleen Arnold stepped in and performed some last minute editing of the book, which elevated its quality. We thank her for that.

We would also want to recognize others whose contribution influenced this book, whether through their perspective, knowledge, and ideas: Tim Durkin, Richard Abernathy, Steve Waldman, George Flint, and Kevin France, for introducing us.

Yoram

I owe a special thank you to my wife, Anat, and my daughters, Maya and Shira, for accepting the time I spent writing and meeting with Lori, on top of running my business. I knew that this time came at your expense, and I appreciate your understanding and support throughout the process. Thank you for laughing at my jokes, even when they weren't so funny… I also want to thank my friends, who advised and supported me through this journey; Mike Bronsky, Ken Gagliano, and Michael Messer.

Lori

I want to thank Yoram for allowing me to go on this journey with him and his patience. Monty, Jadon, and Jenna for their understanding, and especially to Monty for helping me process the many thoughts that ran through my mind as I typed this book. My staff at Vann Counseling & Associates, my parents, Greg and Charlotte, for all of their support throughout my life, my brother, Mark, for serving his country and community on many levels with many sacrifices, my uncle Gary for serving in Vietnam and in the Lewisville School District for decades, and for all of our veterans and their families for the sacrifices that they endure but often go unnoticed.

And most of all, I thank God for the countless opportunities, blessings, people He's placed in my life, the wisdom given, the strength to endure so many situations, and the courage to stand up against the trials of life.

A final note, I would be remiss if I didn't thank my dog, Miss E, for keeping me company each time that I sat down to work on this book, even if she was sleeping or bribed with a bone that kept her busy.

***

To all of you we want to say: we couldn't have done it without you!

The End

About the Authors

Yoram Solomon

Dr. Yoram Solomon is a passionate innovation & strategy thought leader. He published 8 books, 22 patents, and was one of the creators of the Wi-Fi and USB technologies. He was named one of the Top 40 Innovation Bloggers in 2015, 2016, and 2017, and was a columnist at Inc. Magazine, Innovation Excellence, and Dallas Innovates. Dr. Solomon spent years studying why people are creative when they work in startups so much more than when they work in Fortune 500 companies, and earned his PhD for that study. He also holds an MBA and a Law degree.

Yoram is a professor of entrepreneurship at Southern Methodist University; and was a professor of Technology and Industry Forecasting at the Institute for Innovation and Entrepreneurship, the University of Texas at Dallas School of Management; he is active in regional innovation and technology commercialization, and was one of the founding members of the North Texas Angel Network. In 2015 he was elected to the *Plano Independent School District* Board of Trustees, a leading U.S. school district serving 54,000 students in 72 schools. Yoram served in the Israeli Defense Forces 35th Airborne Paratrooper brigade and as a U.S. Air Force CAP pilot and Aerospace Education Officer. He is a professional member of the *National Speakers Association* (NSA) and the *Global Speakers Federation* (GSF).

Additional information can be found on his website:

www.yoramsolomon.com

Lori Vann

Lori Vann is a Licensed Professional Counselor Supervisor who has practiced in a variety of settings from inpatient psychiatric to an outpatient clinic, private practice, and the non-profit sector for the last 20 years. Over the years, she has counseled over 475 individuals who are currently, or have in the past, practiced Non-suicidal Self-injury (NSSI) and consulted on hundreds of cases of self-injury, suicide, abuse, and  ethical issues with her interns and colleagues. Nicknamed the "Guru of self-injury" and regarded as an authority on the issue, she is also considered an expert on professional ethical issues faced by counselors, and called a "Teen Whisperer". Considered a "media darling" for her ability to clearly and concisely articulate information about mental health issues in the news, she has given over 240 interviews for TV, radio, podcasts, and print media formats.

As a professional speaker with almost twenty years of experience and a former college professor, she has presented her years of research at varied locations including national and state conferences, colleges, school districts, hospitals, clinics, and an international educational group. Ms. Vann is currently in the process of writing her fourth book on the subject of self-injury (NSSI) with plans to start penning a book on perfectionism in 2019.

She is a graduate of Pepperdine University, where she received with honors her Bachelor of Arts degree in Psychology and is a graduate of Chapman University, where she graduated Summa Cum Laude with a Master of Arts degree in Psychology with an emphasis in Marriage, Family, and Child Counseling.

Additional information can be found on her websites:
www.LoriVannCounseling.com and www.LoriVannSpeaking.com.

Endnotes

1. *Campus Cautiously Train Freshmen Against Subtle Insults.* The New York Times, 9/6/2016. https://www.nytimes.com/2016/09/07/us/campuses-cautiously-train-freshmen-against-subtle-insults.html

2. *Detroit firefighter fired for bringing watermelon to station.* Fox 2, 10/6/2017. http://www.fox2detroit.com/news/local-news/detroit-firefighter-fired-for-bringing-watermelon-to-station

3. *How Watermelons Became a Racist Trope.* The Atlantic, December 8, 2014. https://www.theatlantic.com/national/archive/2014/12/how-watermelons-became-a-racist-trope/383529/

4. *Black Detroit firefighters defend white recruit fired over watermelon.* News 7 Miami, October 11, 2017. http://wsvn.com/news/us-world/black-detroit-firefighters-defend-white-recruit-fired-over-watermelon/

5. *Home Depot Employee Says He Was Fired After Trying to Stop Kidnapping.* NBC News, July 7, 2017. https://www.nbcnews.com/news/us-news/home-depot-employee-says-he-was-fired-after-trying-stop-n780531

6. *Building Support for Scholarly Practices in Mathematics Methods.* Information Age Publishing, 2017. http://www.infoagepub.com/products/Building-Support-for-Scholarly-Practices-in-Mathematics-Methods

7. *Prof: Algebra, geometry perpetuate white privilege.* Campus Reform, October 23, 2017. https://www.campusreform.org/?ID=10005

8. *Moana, Elsa, and Halloween.* Raising Race Conscious Children, September 2017. http://www.raceconscious.org/2017/09/moana-elsa-halloween/

9. *Halloween as an opportunity to dismantle white supremacy: Three things we believe this Halloween.* Raising Race Conscious Children, October 2017. http://www.raceconscious.org/2017/10/halloween-opportunity-dismantle-white-supremacy-three-things-believe-halloween/

10. *Indian Guides, Princesses must drop Indian theme of leave YMCA.* Chicago Tribune, September 19, 2015. http://www.chicagotribune.com/suburbs/la-grange/news/ct-ymca-indian-princess-met-20150918-story.html

11. *Toronto District School Board to remove 'chief' from job titles* (2017). The Canadian Press. http://nationalpost.com/pmn/news-pmn/canada-news-pmn/toronto-district-school-board-to-remove-chief-from-all-job-titles

12. David Zahniser (2017). *L.A. City Council replaces Columbus Day with Indigenous Peoples Day on city calendar.* http://www.latimes.com/local/lanow/la-me-ln-indigenous-peoples-day-20170829-story.html

13 Matthew Haag (2017). *ESPN Pulls Announcer Robert Lee From Virginia Game Because of His Name.* https://www.nytimes.com/2017/08/23/business/media/robert-lee-university-virginia-charlottesville.html

14 Philip Jankowski (2017). *Austin City Council replaces Columbus Day with Indigenous Peoples Day.* Austin American-Statesman. http://www.mystatesman.com/news/local/austin-city-council-replaces-columbus-day-with-indigenous-peoples-day/rZ1Av73XMe1C5ZkUxO3UtL/

15 Emily Zanotti (2017). *George Washington's Church Will REMOVE Plaque Honoring First President.* The Daily Wire. http://www.dailywire.com/news/22885/george-washingtons-church-will-remove-plaque-emily-zanotti#

16 Hannah Lang (2017). *Court: Cross-shaped WWI memorial is unconstitutional.* CNN. http://www.cnn.com/2017/10/19/politics/maryland-cross-monument-unconstitutional/index.html

17 Adam Sabes (2018). *Purdue writing guide: Words with 'MAN' 'should be avoided'.* Campus Reform. https://www.campusreform.org/?ID=10539

18 Shanna Nelson (2017). Student has grade docked for using 'mankind' in English paper. Campus Reform. https://www.campusreform.org/?ID=8986

19 *Political Correctness, Definition.* Oxford Living Dictionaries. https://en.oxforddictionaries.com/definition/political_correctness

20 Gregg Henriques, PhD (2016). *Theory of Knowledge. Psychology Today. Political Correctness Unpacked—A brief essay unpacking PC.* Psychology Today. https://www.psychologytoday.com/blog/theory-knowledge/201601/political-correctness-unpacked

21 Joshua Florence (2015). *A Phrase in Flux: The History of Political Correctness.* Harvard Political Review. http://harvardpolitics.com/united-states/phrase-flux-history-political-correctness/

22 *The Origins of Political Correctness* (2000). Accuracy in Academia. https://www.academia.org/the-origins-of-political-correctness/

23 Angelo M. Codevilla (2016). *THE RISE OF POLITICAL CORRECTNESS.* http://www.claremont.org/crb/article/the-rise-of-political-correctness/

24 *Political Correctness Wanted Dead or Alive* (2016). Talk Decoded. https://www.talkdecoded.com/blog/2016/11/29/political-correctness-wanted-dead-or-alive

25 Hannah Fingerhut (2016). *In 'political correctness' debate, most Americans think too many people are easily offended.* Pew Research Center.

http://www.pewresearch.org/fact-tank/2016/07/20/in-political-correctness-debate-most-americans-think-too-many-people-are-easily-offended/

[26] *Fox News Poll: September 28, 2017.* Fox News. http://www.foxnews.com/politics/interactive/2017/09/28/fox-news-poll-september-28-2017.html

[27] *73% Say Freedom of Speech Worth Dying For* (2017). Rasmussen Reports. http://www.rasmussenreports.com/public_content/lifestyle/general_lifestyle/august_2017/73_say_freedom_of_speech_worth_dying_for

[28] Ann Pietrangelo (2017). *Left Brain vs. Right Brain: What Does This Mean for Me?* Health line. https://www.healthline.com/health/left-brain-vs-right-brain#takeaway5

[29] Tania Lombrozo (2013). *The Truth About The Left Brain / Right Brain Relationship.* NPR/KERA. http://www.npr.org/sections/13.7/2013/12/02/248089436/the-truth-about-the-left-brain-right-brain-relationship

[30] Nagesh Belludi (2008). *Albert Mehrabian's 7-38-55 Rule of Personal Communication.* Right Attitudes. http://www.rightattitudes.com/2008/10/04/7-38-55-rule-personal-communication/

[31] Barbara L. Fredrickson . *Positive Emotions Broaden and Build.* University of North Carolina at Chapel Hill. http://www.unc.edu/peplab/publications/Fredrickson_AESP_final.pdf

[32] *Janus, Roman God* (2018). Encyclopedia Britannica. https://www.britannica.com/topic/Janus-Roman-god

[33] Bryan Cross (2014). *Clark, Frame, and the Analogy of Painting a Magisterial Target Around One's Interpretive Arrow.* Called to Communion. http://www.calledtocommunion.com/2014/01/clark-frame-and-the-analogy-of-painting-a-magisterial-target-around-ones-interpretive-arrow/

[34] Paul Krugman (2013). *Incestuous Amplification, Economics Edition.* The Conscience of a Liberal. The New York Times. https://krugman.blogs.nytimes.com/2013/01/29/incestuousamplification-economics-edition/

[35] Robert Cialdini (1993). *Influence: Science and practice.* New York: HarperCollinsCollegePublishers

[36] http://www.dictionary.com/browse/conservative; http://www.dictionary.com/browse/liberal?s=t; http://www.dictionary.com/browse/progressive?s=t; https://www.oxfordlearnersdictionaries.com/us/definition/english/conservative_1?q=conservative;

https://www.oxfordlearnersdictionaries.com/us/definition/english/liberal_1?q=liberal; https://www.oxfordlearnersdictionaries.com/us/definition/english/progressive_1?q=progressive; https://www.merriam-webster.com/dictionary/conservative; https://www.merriam-webster.com/dictionary/liberal; https://www.merriam-webster.com/dictionary/progressive

[37] *How Many Possible Combinations Of DNA Are There?* (2017). Forbes. https://www.forbes.com/sites/quora/2017/01/20/how-many-possible-combinations-of-dna-are-there/#2999f2fd5835

[38] Shahram Heshmat. *What is Confirmation Bias? Wishful thinking.* (2015). Psychology Today. https://www.psychologytoday.com/blog/science-choice/201504/what-is-confirmation-bias

[39] Vanessa Otero, *The Media Bias Chart.* (2017) http://www.allgeneralizationsarefalse.com/

[40] Yoram Solomon (2017). *Culture starts with YOU, not your boss!* CreateSpace Publishing. https://www.largescalecreativity.com/culture-starts-with-you-not-your-boss/

[41] A phrase often used to describe that employees prefer to "go with the flow" instead of taking risks, to protect their jobs, believing that if they take risks and fail, they will suffer significant consequences.

[42] *Definition of Heuristic.* Merriam Webster Dictionary. https://www.merriam-webster.com/dictionary/heuristic

[43] Mackey, J., & Sisodia, R. (2013). *Conscious capitalism: liberating the heroic spirit of business.* Boston, Mass.: Harvard Business Review Press.

[44] Ariana Brockington. (2017) *Home Depot Employee Says He Was Fired After Trying to Stop Kidnapping.* NBC News. https://www.nbcnews.com/news/us-news/home-depot-employee-says-he-was-fired-after-trying-stop-n780531

[45] *Voting Records.* govtrack. https://www.govtrack.us/congress/votes

[46] Available from MIT under the *Creative Commons Attribution License*

[47] Andris C, Lee D, Hamilton MJ, Martino M, Gunning CE, Selden JA (2015) *The Rise of Partisanship and Super-Cooperators in the U.S. House of Representatives.* PLoS ONE 10(4): e0123507. doi:10.1371/journal.pone.0123507 http://senseable.mit.edu/papers/pdf/20150421_Andris_etal_RisePartisanship_PlosOne.pdf

[48] *Fox News Poll: September 28, 2017.* http://www.foxnews.com/politics/interactive/2017/09/28/fox-news-poll-september-28-2017.html

49 Ornstein, Mann, Malbin, Rugg and Wakeman (2016). *Vital Statistics on Congress*. https://www.brookings.edu/wp-content/uploads/2017/01/vitalstats_ch6_full.pdf

50 Pew Research Center, U.S. Politics & Policy. Beyond Distrust: How Americans View Their Government. http://www.people-press.org/2015/11/23/beyond-distrust-how-americans-view-their-government/

51 We are using the term "party line" loosely here. While the Senate votes on these two legislative pieces were along party lines, the votes that took place in the house didn't have any support from the minority party, but suffered some opposition from the majority party, albeit not enough to stop them.

52 John Gramlich (2017). *Far more Americans say there are strong conflicts between partisans than between other groups in society*. Pew Research Center. http://www.pewresearch.org/fact-tank/2017/12/19/far-more-americans-say-there-are-strong-conflicts-between-partisans-than-between-other-groups-in-society/

53 Laura Paisley (2016). *Political polarization at its worst since the Civil War*. USC News. https://news.usc.edu/110124/political-polarization-at-its-worst-since-the-civil-war-2/

54 Hannah Fingerhut (2018). *Why do people belong to a party? Negative views of the opposing party are a major factor*. PEW Research Center. http://www.pewresearch.org/fact-tank/2018/03/29/why-do-people-belong-to-a-party-negative-views-of-the-opposing-party-are-a-major-factor/

55 Heather Rudow (2013). *Resolution of EMU case confirms ACA Code of Ethics, counseling profession's stance against client discrimination*. Counseling Today. http://ct.counseling.org/2013/01/resolution-of-emu-case-confirms-aca-code-of-ethics-counseling-professions-stance-against-client-discrimination/

56 Heather Rudow (2013). *Resolution of EMU case confirms ACA Code of Ethics, counseling profession's stance against client discrimination*. Counseling Today. http://ct.counseling.org/2013/01/resolution-of-emu-case-confirms-aca-code-of-ethics-counseling-professions-stance-against-client-discrimination/

57 Michelle R. Cox (2013). *When religion and sexual orientation collide*. Counseling Today. http://ct.counseling.org/2013/05/when-religion-and-sexual-orientation-collide

58 *When religion and sexual orientation collide*. http://ct.counseling.org/2013/05/when-religion-and-sexual-orientation-collide

59 *Farm Demographics - U.S. Farmers by Gender, Age, Race, Ethnicity, and More*. 2012 Census Highlights https://www.agcensus.usda.gov/Publications/2012/Online_Resources/Highlights/Farm_Demographics/

60 *Employment by major industry sector* (2017). Bureau of Labor Statistics. https://www.bls.gov/emp/ep_table_201.htm

61 *Snowflake, definition* (2017). Urban Dictionary. https://www.urbandictionary.com/define.php?term=Snowflake.

62 Jag Bhalla. *It's In Our Nature To Need Rules. Big Think.* http://bigthink.com/errors-we-live-by/it-is-in-our-nature-to-need-rules

63 Simi Agarwal (2010). *Why Some Human Brains Become Leaders, While Others Followers?* NEUROSCIENCE & NEUROLOGY. http://brainblogger.com/2010/03/06/why-some-human-brains-become-leaders-while-others-followers/

64 Kathy Caprino (2014). 7 Crippling Parenting Behaviors That Keep Children From Growing Into Leaders. https://www.forbes.com/sites/kathycaprino/2014/01/16/7-crippling-parenting-behaviors-that-keep-children-from-growing-into-leaders/#257741a75957

65 Diana Simeon. *Why Helicopter Parenting is (Really) Bad for Teenagers.* YOUR TEEN for parents. https://yourteenmag.com/family-life/helicopter-parents-2

66 Lenore Skenazy & Jonathan Haidt (2017). *The Fragile Generation: Bad policy and paranoid parenting are making kids too safe to succeed.* http://reason.com/archives/2017/10/26/the-fragile-generation

67 Liz Farmer (2017). *2 teens killed, 1 injured when Porsche crashes into tree, catches fire in Plano.* The Dallas Morning News. https://www.dallasnews.com/news/plano/2017/02/11/2-teens-killed-1-injured-porsche-crashes-tree-catches-fire-plano-police-say

68 *Graduated Driver License (GDL) Program.* Texas Department of Public Safety. https://www.dps.texas.gov/DriverLicense/gdl.htm

69 Caila Klass & Alexa Waliente (2015). *'Affluenza' DUI Case: What Happened Night of the Accident That Left 4 People Dead.* ABC News. http://abcnews.go.com/US/affluenza-dui-case-happened-night-accident-left-people/story?id=34481444

70 *Ethan Couch.* Wikipedia. https://en.wikipedia.org/wiki/Ethan_Couch

71 Jenner Smith (2018). 'Affluenza teen' Ethan Couch expected to be released from jail. ABC News. http://abcnews.go.com/US/affluenza-teen-ethan-couch-expected-released-jail/story?id=54130494

72 Evan Grossman. *How Participation Trophies Are Making Our Kids Soft.* Men's Journal. https://www.mensjournal.com/adventure/how-participation-trophies-are-making-our-kids-soft-20150725/

73 Betty Berdan (2016). *Participation Trophies Send a Dangerous Message*. The New York Times. https://www.nytimes.com/roomfordebate/2016/10/06/should-every-young-athlete-get-a-trophy/participation-trophies-send-a-dangerous-message

74 Evan Grossman. *How Participation Trophies Are Making Our Kids Soft*. Men's Journal. https://www.mensjournal.com/adventure/how-participation-trophies-are-making-our-kids-soft-20150725/

75 *Affirmative Action*. ACLU. https://www.aclu.org/issues/racial-justice/affirmative-action

76 Becky Little (2017). *Why the DOJ is Suing Colleges on Behalf of White Students*. The History Channel. http://www.history.com/news/the-landmark-supreme-court-case-that-upheld-affirmative-action

77 Ron Marshall (2015). *How Many Ads Do You See in One Day?* Red Crow Marketing, Inc. https://www.redcrowmarketing.com/2015/09/10/many-ads-see-one-day/

78 Chris Cillizza (2014). *Just 7 percent of journalists are Republicans. That's far fewer than even a decade ago*. The Washington Post.

79 Jack Shafer & Tucker Doherty (2017). *The Media Bubble Is Worse Than You Think*. POLITICO Magazine. https://www.politico.com/magazine/story/2017/04/25/media-bubble-real-journalism-jobs-east-coast-215048

80 Chanelle Ignant (2016). *How Does Social Media Shape Our Political Views?* KQED Education. https://ww2.kqed.org/education/2016/10/21/how-does-social-media-shape-our-political-views/

81 Ben Riely-Smith (2018). *Ex-Google and Facebook staff warn of social media dangers*. The Telegraph. http://www.telegraph.co.uk/news/2018/02/05/ex-google-facebook-staff-warn-social-media-dangers/

82 *The Fragile Generation*

83 *The Fragile Generation*

84 Lori Vann (2015). *A Practitioner's Training in the Treatment of Self-injury: tips, techniques, activities, and debates*. Audio CD.

85 Ramin Mojtabai, Mark Olfson & Beth Han (2016). *National Trends in the Prevalence and Treatment of Depression in Adolescents and Young Adults*. Pediatrics. http://pediatrics.aappublications.org/content/early/2016/11/10/peds.2016-1878

86 Christopher Johnson MD (2017). *Why Are Suicide Rates Rising? Completed attempts are just the tip of the iceberg*. MEDPAGE Today. https://www.medpagetoday.com/blogs/kevinmd/64557

87 *Suicide* (2017). National Institute of Mental Health. https://www.nimh.nih.gov/health/statistics/suicide.shtml

[88] Drapeau, C. W., & McIntosh, J. L. (for the American Association of Suicidology). (2016). U.S.A. suicide 2015: Official final data. Washington, DC: American Association of Suicidology, dated December 23, 2016, downloaded from http://www.suicidology.org.)

[89] *Does YOUR child self-harm? Then you have a 12-month window to stop suicide, experts say* (2017). The Daily Mail. http://www.dailymail.co.uk/health/article-4335400/Does-child-selfharm-1-year-stop-suicide.html)

[90] Christopher Johnson (2017). *Why Are Suicide Rates Rising? Completed attempts are just the tip of the iceberg.* MedPage Today. https://www.medpagetoday.com/blogs/kevinmd/64557

[91] Natasha Tracy (2016). *SELF-HARM AND SUICIDE: CAN SELF-INJURY LEAD TO SUICIDE?* Healthy Place. https://www.healthyplace.com/abuse/self-injury/self-harm-and-suicide-can-self-injury-lead-to-suicide/

[92] *SAMHSA report shows increase in opioid treatment facilities* (2017). Substance Abuse and Mental Health Services Administration. https://www.samhsa.gov/newsroom/press-announcements/201708220100

[93] *Treatment for Substance Use Disorders* (2018). Drug War Facts. http://www.drugwarfacts.org/chapter/treatment

[94] Keith Perry (2014). *Watching violent films does make people more aggressive, study shows.* The Telegraph. http://www.telegraph.co.uk/news/science/11087683/Watching-violent-films-does-make-people-more-aggressive-study-shows.html

[95] Dale Archer (2013). *Violence, The Media and Your Brain. How media violence from movies to TV to video games adversely affects the brain.* Psychology Today. https://www.psychologytoday.com/blog/reading-between-the-headlines/201309/violence-the-media-and-your-brain

[96] *Authority, Definition.* Merriam-Webster Dictionary. https://www.merriam-webster.com/dictionary/authority

[97] Saul McLeod (2017). *Maslow's Hierarchy of Needs.* Simply Psychology. https://www.simplypsychology.org/maslow.html

[98] Saul McLeod (2007). *The Milgram Experiment.* Simply Psychology. https://www.simplypsychology.org/milgram.html

[99] *The Milgram Experiment.*

[100] Saul McLeod (2008). *Hofling Hospital Experiment.* Simply Psychology. https://www.simplypsychology.org/hofling-obedience.html

[101] C.S. Lewis (1952). *Mere Christianity.* https://github.com/F1LT3R/mere-christianity/blob/master/book-3/Mere-Christianity-Book-3.-Christian-Behaviour.md

[102] *Why the decline in the number of listed American firms matters. Company founders are reluctant to go public and takeovers are soaring* (2017). The Economist. https://www.economist.com/news/business/21721153-company-founders-are-reluctant-go-public-and-takeovers-are-soaring-why-decline

[103] *Las Vegas shooting: This is what investigators found in Stephen Paddock's hotel room* (2018). ABC 15, Arizona. https://www.abc15.com/news/las-vegas-shooting/list-guns-and-evidence-from-las-vegas-shooter-stephen-paddock

[104] Sean Davis (2017). *Here Are The Actual Federal Laws Regulating Machine Guns In The U.S.* The Federalist. http://thefederalist.com/2017/10/02/actual-federal-laws-regulating-machine-guns-u-s/

[105] *Firearms - Guides - Importation & Verification of Firearms - National Firearms Act Definitions – Machinegun.* Bureau of Alcohol, Tobacco, Firearms and Explosives. https://www.atf.gov/firearms/firearms-guides-importation-verification-firearms-national-firearms-act-definitions-0

[106] *What Is a Bump Stock and How Does It Work?* (2018). The New York Times. https://www.nytimes.com/interactive/2017/10/04/us/bump-stock-las-vegas-gun.html

[107] Christal Hayes (2017). *Las Vegas gunman Stephen Paddock fired 1,100 bullets during rampage, forensics report finds.* Newsweek. http://www.newsweek.com/las-vegas-gunman-fired-1100-bullets-during-shooting-new-forensic-report-finds-723311

[108] Jeremiah Cottle (2012). *Method of shooting a semi-automatic firearm. United States Patent 8,127,658.* U.S. Patent and Trademark Office. http://www.freepatentsonline.com/8127658.html

[109] *The Fine Print—Read It.* Truth in Advertising. https://www.truthinadvertising.org/the-law-of-fine-print/

[110] *Plausable Deniability Law and Legal Definition.* US Legal. https://definitions.uslegal.com/p/plausable-deniability/

[111] *Zero Tolerance.* The Free dictionary. https://legal-dictionary.thefreedictionary.com/zero+tolerance

[112] Frank LoMonte (2012). *Zero Tolerance for Online Bullying Can Hamper Free Speech.* American Bar Association. https://www.americanbar.org/groups/litigation/committees/childrens-rights/articles/2012/zero-tolerance-online-bullying-can-hamper-free-speech.html

113 *Jumpstart Our Business Startups (JOBS) Act.* U.S. Securities and Exchange Commission. https://www.sec.gov/spotlight/jobs-act.shtml

114 *Regulation Crowdfunding: A Small Entity Compliance Guide for Issuers* (2017). U.S. Securities and Exchange Commission. https://www.sec.gov/info/smallbus/secg/rccomplianceguide-051316.htm

115 Donelson R. Forsyth (2008). *Group Dynamics.* https://facultystaff.richmond.edu/~dforsyth/pubs/forsyth2008.pdf

116 *What is Groupthink?* PsySR. http://www.psysr.org/about/pubs_resources/groupthink%20overview.htm

117 Joseph M. Carver. *Love and Stockholm Syndrome: The Mystery of Loving an Abuser.* Counselling Resource. https://counsellingresource.com/therapy/self-help/stockholm

118 *Frank Stephens' Opening Statement on Down Syndrome* (2017). C-SPAN. https://www.c-span.org/video/?c4687834/frank-stephens-opening-statement-syndrome

119 *Civil Lawsuit Statistics.* Statistic Brain. 9/3/2016. https://www.statisticbrain.com/civil-lawsuit-statistics/

120 *International Comparisons of Litigation Costs, June 2013 Update.* U.S. Chamber Institute for Legal Reform. http://www.instituteforlegalreform.com/uploads/sites/1/ILR_NERA_Study_International_Liability_Costs-update.pdf

121 *The World Factbook.* Central Intelligence Agency. https://www.cia.gov/library/publications/the-world-factbook/rankorder/2004rank.html

122 *GDP per capita.* The World Bank. https://data.worldbank.org/indicator/NY.GDP.PCAP.CD

123 *2011 Update on U.S. Tort Cost Trends* (2012). Willis Towers Watson. https://www.towerswatson.com/en/Insights/IC-Types/Survey-Research-Results/2012/01/2011-Update-on-US-Tort-Cost-Trends

124 *Medical liability costs in U.S. pegged at 2.4 percent of annual health care spending* (2010). Harvard School of Public Health. https://www.hsph.harvard.edu/news/press-releases/medical-liability-costs-us/

125 *2015 Litigation Trends Annual Survey.* Norton Rose Fulbright. http://www.nortonrosefulbright.com/files/20150514-2015-litigation-trends-survey_v24-128746.pdf

[126] *How Many Lawsuits are There in the U.S. & What are They For? An Amazing Overview.* SixWise. http://www.sixwise.com/newsletters/06/10/05/how-many-lawsuits-are-there-in-the-us--amp-what-are-they-for-an-amazing-overview.htm

[127] Minh N. Vu, Kristina M. Launey & Susan Ryan (2017). *ADA Title III Lawsuits Increase by 37 Percent in 2016.* Seyfarth Shaw LLP. https://www.adatitleiii.com/2017/01/ada-title-iii-lawsuits-increase-by-37-percent-in-2016/

[128] *McDonalds' Hot Coffee Case - Read the Facts NOT the Fiction.* Center for Justice & Democracy. Texas Trial Lawyers Association. https://www.ttla.com/index.cfm?pg=McDonaldsCoffeeCaseFacts

[129] Jacqulyn Powell (2017). *Woman who drove off parking garage suing for $1M.* KXAN. http://kxan.com/2017/08/23/woman-files-lawsuit-after-driving-off-downtown-parking-garage/

[130] *The Facts of Pearson v. Chung* (2008). Manning Sossamon.https://web.archive.org/web/20090515122156/http://manning-sossamon.com/pantfacts/

[131] *We, The Plaintiffs. A Closer Look at America's Obsession with Lawsuits.* eLocal-Lawyers. https://abovethelaw.com/uploads/2012/07/WethePlaintiffs2.jpg

[132] Matt Leichter. *Lawyers per Capita by State.* The Last Gen X American. https://lawschooltuitionbubble.wordpress.com/original-research-updated/lawyers-per-capita-by-state/

[133] *United States Population, 1900-2017.* Trading Economics. https://tradingeconomics.com/united-states/population

[134] *Measuring America: The Decennial Census from 1790 to 2000* (2002). U.S. Census Bureau. https://www.census.gov/history/pdf/measuringamerica.pdf

[135] *American Bar Association National Lawyer Population Survey. Historical Trend in Total National Lawyer Population, 1878-2017.* American Bar Association. https://www.americanbar.org/content/dam/aba/administrative/market_research/Total%20National%20Lawyer%20Population%201878-2017.authcheckdam.pdf

[136] *State of the Congress 2013.* Measure of America of the Social Science Research Council. http://www.measureofamerica.org/113-congress-infographic/

[137] *First Year and Total J.D. Enrollment by Gender 1947-2011.* American Bar Association. https://www.americanbar.org/content/dam/aba/administrative/legal_education_and_admissions_to_the_bar/statistics/jd_enrollment_1yr_total_gender.authcheckdam.pdf

[138] Jennifer Smith (2013). *Law-school matriculation plunges to 1970s levels*. Market Watch. https://www.marketwatch.com/story/law-school-enrollment-plunges-to-1970s-levels-2013-12-17

[139] Ilana Kowarski (2017). *Less Competitive Law School Admissions a Boon for Applicants*. U.S.News. https://www.usnews.com/education/best-graduate-schools/top-law-schools/articles/2017-08-08/law-school-admissions-less-competitive-than-2008

[140] *120 Years of American Education: A Statistical Portrait* (1993). U.S. Department of Education, the National Center for Education Statistics: https://nces.ed.gov/pubs93/93442.pdf

[141] The People History: 1960s Important News and Events, Key Technology Fashion and Popular Culture. http://www.thepeoplehistory.com/1960s.html

[142] Chuck Underwood. *The Generational Imperative*. 2007. Book Surge. North Charleston, South Carolina.

[143] *The Names of Vietnam War Personnel, 1945 To 1975*. The American War Library. http://www.americanwarlibrary.com/vietnam/vwatl.htm

[144] *Fact vs. Fiction….. The Vietnam Veteran*. Vietnam and All Veterans of Florida State Coalition. http://www.vvof.org/factsvnv.htm

[145] *Vietnam War U.S. Military Fatal Casualty Statistics*. National Archives. https://www.archives.gov/research/military/vietnam-war/casualty-statistics

[146] *Number of TV Households in America*. The Buffalo History Museum. http://www.buffalohistory.org/Explore/Exhibits/virtual_exhibits/wheels_of_power/educ_materials/television_handout.pdf

[147] *Background of Selective Service*. U.S. Selective Service System. https://www.sss.gov/About/History-And-Records/Background-Of-Selective-Service

[148] *Induction Statistics*. U.S. Selective Service System. https://www.sss.gov/About/History-And-Records/Induction-Statistics

[149] *Richard Nixon, Executive Order 11497—Amending the Selective Service Regulations to Prescribe Random Selection*. The American Presidency Project, University of California Santa Barbara. http://www.presidency.ucsb.edu/ws/?pid=106002

[150] *The Vietnam Lotteries*. U.S. Selective Service System. https://www.sss.gov/About/History-And-Records/lotter1

[151] *The Vietnam Lotteries*.

[152] *The Vietnam Lotteries*.

[153] Were at the right age and health required to serve.

154 *CBS News Lottery Draft – 1969*. YouTube. https://www.youtube.com/watch?v=-p5X1FjyD_g

155 Robert S. Erikson & Laura Stoker (2010). *Caught in the Draft: Vietnam Draft Lottery Status and Political Attitudes*. Columbia University. http://www.columbia.edu/~rse14/vietnam_rev_Feb2010.pdf

156 *Caught in the Draft*

157 Sarena F. Goodman and Adam M. Isen (2015). *Un-Fortunate Sons: Effects of the Vietnam Draft Lottery on the Next Generation's Labor Market*. Federal Reserve Board, Washington D.C. https://www.federalreserve.gov/econres/feds/files/2015119r1pap.pdf

158 *Classifications*. U.S. Selective Service System. https://www.sss.gov/Classifications

159 *Women in the Vietnam War*. The History Channel. http://www.history.com/topics/vietnam-war/women-in-the-vietnam-war

160 Blake Stilwell. *11 ways people dodged the Vietnam draft*. We are the Mighty. http://www.wearethemighty.com/articles/vietnam-draft-dodger

161 Bill Lind (2000). *The Origins of Political Correctness*. Accuracy in Academia. https://www.academia.org/the-origins-of-political-correctness/

162 *Resistance and Revolution: The Anti-Vietnam War Movement at the University of Michigan, 1965-1972*. University of Michigan. http://michiganintheworld.history.lsa.umich.edu/antivietnamwar/

163 *Legal Trends Report, 2017*. Clio, Themis Solutions Inc. https://files.goclio.com/marketo/ebooks/2017-Legal-Trends-Report.pdf

164 *Consumer Price Index 1913-*. Federal Reserve Bank of Minneapolis. https://www.minneapolisfed.org/community/teaching-aids/cpi-calculator-information/consumer-price-index-and-inflation-rates-1913

165 Sara Randazzo and Jacqueline Palank (2016). *Legal Fees Cross New Mark: $1,500 an Hour*. The Wall Street Journal. https://www.wsj.com/articles/legal-fees-reach-new-pinnacle-1-500-an-hour-1454960708

166 *2015 Hourly Fact Sheet* (2016). State Bar of Texas Department of Research and Analysis. https://www.texasbar.com/AM/Template.cfm?Section=Demographic_and_Economic_Trends&Template=/CM/ContentDisplay.cfm&ContentID=34182

167 Gretchen Morgenson & Louise Story (2009). *Banks Bundled Bad Debt, Bet Against It and Won*. http://www.nytimes.com/2009/12/24/business/24trading.html?pagewanted=all

[168] Jessica Pressler (2009). *Bad News Bears: The Guys Who Bet Against the Bubble and Won*. New York Magazine. http://nymag.com/daily/intelligencer/2009/11/bad_news_bears_2.html

[169] *Short Selling*. Investopedia. https://www.investopedia.com/terms/s/shortselling.asp

[170] *Hedge Fund*. Investopedia. https://www.investopedia.com/terms/h/hedgefund.asp

[171] *Big Data: The growth of the hedge fund industry* (2015). HedgeFund Intelligence. https://www.aima.org/uploads/assets/uploaded/4bfc8865-47a8-435e-8fb07cddc98ffb4b.pdf

[172] *Bitcoin (USD) Price*. Coindesk. https://www.coindesk.com/price/

[173] Chicago Board Options Exchange

[174] *XBT-CBOE Bitcoin Futures*. CBOE. http://cfe.cboe.com/cfe-products/xbt-cboe-bitcoin-futures

[175] Evelyn Cheng (2017). *Bitcoin futures surge more than 19% during first day of trading*. CNBC. https://www.cnbc.com/2017/12/10/bitcoin-futures-set-to-trade-on-cboe-sunday-evening.html

[176] Michelle Fox. *People are taking out mortgages to buy bitcoin, says securities regulator*. CNBC, December 11, 2017. https://www.cnbc.com/2017/12/11/people-are-taking-out-mortgages-to-buy-bitcoin-says-joseph-borg.html

[177] *How Do I Get the Other Side to Pay My Attorney Fees if I Win a Lawsuit?* HG.org Legal Resources. https://www.hg.org/article.asp?id=31422

[178] *Defending the Frivolous Lawsuit: Can You Recover Your Legal Fees?* JD Supra. https://www.jdsupra.com/legalnews/defending-the-frivolous-lawsuit-can-yo-81263/

[179] *Roy L. PEARSON, Jr., Appellant, v. Soo CHUNG, et al., Appellees*. Case No. 07-CV-872 in the District of Columbia Court of Appeals. http://caselaw.findlaw.com/dc-court-of-appeals/1339256.html

[180] *Court Rules for Cleaners in $54 Million Pants Suit*. The Washington Post, June 25, 2007. http://www.washingtonpost.com/wp-dyn/content/article/2007/06/25/AR2007062500443.html

[181] *101 Dumbest Moments in Business. #37: Judge Roy Pearson*. Fortune, January 16, 2008. http://archive.fortune.com/galleries/2007/fortune/0712/gallery.101_dumbest.fortune/37.html

[182] *Litigation Cost Survey of Major Companies*. Submitted by Lawyers for Civil Justice, Civil Justice Reform Group, U.S. Chamber Institute for Legal Reform. 2010 Conference on Civil Litigation.

http://www.uscourts.gov/sites/default/files/litigation_cost_survey_of_major_companies_0.pdf

[183] *Usury Laws*. Investopedia. http://www.investopedia.com/terms/u/usury-laws.asp

[184] American Legal Finance Association. https://americanlegalfin.com/

[185] ALFA Member Companies. https://americanlegalfin.com/alfa-membership/alfa-member-companies/

[186] Binyamin Appelbaum. *Lawsuit Loans Add New Risk for the Injured*. The New York Times, January 16, 2001. http://www.nytimes.com/2011/01/17/business/17lawsuit.html

[187] The Center for Public Integrity. https://www.publicintegrity.org/

[188] *About Us*. Budford Capital, LLC. http://www.burfordcapital.com/about/

[189] *The Business of Litigation Finance Is Booming*. Bloomberg Businessweek. May 30, 2017. https://www.bloomberg.com/news/articles/2017-05-30/the-business-of-litigation-finance-is-booming

[190] *2017 Litigation Finance Survey*. Burford Capital, LLC. http://www.burfordcapital.com/2017-litigation-finance-survey/

[191] The last two lines are very consistent with Binyamin Appelbaum's statement that the litigation financing firms would fund just about 10% of the claim value.

[192] *Barratry*. Legal Dictionary, The Free Dictionary. http://legal-dictionary.thefreedictionary.com/barratry

[193] Victor Li (2017). *Legal advertising blows past $1 billion and goes viral*. ABA Journal. http://www.abajournal.com/magazine/article/legal_advertising_viral_video

[194] *Civil Lawsuit Statistics*. Statistic Brain. 9/3/2016. https://www.statisticbrain.com/civil-lawsuit-statistics/

[195] Paul Barrett. *The Business of Litigation Finance Is Booming*. Bloomberg Business week, May 30, 2017. https://www.bloomberg.com/news/articles/2017-05-30/the-business-of-litigation-finance-is-booming

[196] Chris Gallant. *What is securitization?* Investopedia, November 1, 2017. https://www.investopedia.com/ask/answers/07/securitization.asp?lgl=myfinance-layout-no-ads

[197] *Searching for an alternative investment?* Pravati Capital. https://pravaticapital.com/alternative-investments/

[198] *We make investing in litigation simple*. LexShares. https://www.lexshares.com/pages/investors

[199] *Civil Lawsuit Statistics*. Statistic Brain, September 3, 2016. https://www.statisticbrain.com/civil-lawsuit-statistics/

[200] Jonathan Berr. *Shrinking Law Schools Face Financial Devastation*. The Fiscal Times, March 13, 2014. http://www.thefiscaltimes.com/Articles/2014/03/13/Shrinking-Law-Schools-Face-Financial-Devastation

[201] Daniel O. Bernstine. *The State of Law School Admissions: Where Are We in 2014?* The Bar Examiner, June 2014. https://www.aals.org/wp-content/uploads/2014/08/State-of-Law-School-Admissions-2014.pdf

[202] George Orwell, *1984*. Harvill Secker, 1949.

[203] *Military Awards for Valor – Top 3*. U.S. Department of Defense. http://valor.defense.gov/Description-of-Awards/

[204] The Computer, Machine of the Year (1983) .Time Magazine. http://content.time.com/time/covers/0,16641,19830103,00.html

[205] *Gun Violence: How The U.S. Compares With Other Countries*. NPR, October 6, 2017. https://www.npr.org/sections/goatsandsoda/2017/10/06/555861898/gun-violence-how-the-u-s-compares-to-other-countries, and *GBD Compare | Viz Hub*. Institute for Health Metrics and Evaluation, University of Washington, 2018. https://vizhub.healthdata.org/gbd-compare/

[206] *Selected Findings from PISA 2015*. National Center for Education Statistics. https://nces.ed.gov/surveys/pisa/pisa2015/pisa2015highlights_1.asp

[207] The numbers were taken from: Paul Zak (2017). *The Neuroscience of Trust*. Harvard Business Review. https://hbr.org/2017/01/the-neuroscience-of-trust

[208] *America is NOT the Greatest Country Anymore* – HBO Newsroom. https://www.youtube.com/watch?v=VMqcLUqYqrs

[209] Aaron Sorkin. *The Newsroom Script, Episode 1*. Goodreads. https://www.goodreads.com/work/quotes/23633463-the-newsroom-script-episode-1

[210] Newsroom: *The Idealist vs. The Realist*. https://www.youtube.com/watch?v=ZUQJKMngrYo

[211] *We Just Decided To*. The Newsroom S01e01 Episode Script. https://www.springfieldspringfield.co.uk/view_episode_scripts.php?tv-show=the-newsroom&episode=s01e01